Dear Patient

A practical guide to patient experience

Kunle Thomas

Top Agenda Publishing UK
London

Published in the United Kingdom by Top Agenda Publishing UK, London.

ISBN: 978-0-9556505-2-9

Hardcover ISBN: 978-0-9556505-4-3

E-book ISBN: 978-0-9556505-3-6

Cover design: Daniel Ojedokun (@danny_media, fiverr)

Layout design and formatting: Jbookdesigns (@josepepitojr, fiverr)

Author photographed by Snappy Snaps, Kingsway, London WC2 (applicable to hardcover only)

This book is dedicated to all those working in the UK and across the globe to ensure the patient's voice is heard, especially the voice of vulnerable patients/ service users.

FOREWORD

In the founding speech for the NHS on 5th July 1948, Health Minister Aneurin Bevan MP was able to confirm the work of several years and numerous lobbyists by boiling everything down to 3 principles: The National Health Service should help everyone, the healthcare provided should be free, and that care would be provided based on need rather than ability to pay.

Perhaps he should have added another - that the service design should start with the patient and work backwards.

That I am having to write this in 2023, as we celebrate 75 years of the NHS, is a difficult but important observation. To my eye and in my experience, a publicly funded service that rightly attracts great respect and affection from the general public, is too often not designed from the patient's start point.

Back in 1948, health needs were different. Obesity was unusual in post-war Britain and so was diabetes, as were many other long-term conditions you might recognise now, and which take huge amounts of NHS budget. Health inequalities were certainly obvious, but the dire consequences of societal breakdown and drug abuse less so. Mental health interventions were rudimentary and probably barbaric by today's standards but the idea of children and young people self-harming and experiencing an eating disorder epidemic would have been dismissed. Residential and domiciliary social care provision was in its infancy and the scale of the sector as it is now would astonish time travellers.

But many of our systems, structures and processes remain unchanged, particularly the chasm between health and social care provision. And given that many patients present with multiple conditions and complex domestic and societal needs, there is now a labyrinth for patients to navigate if they are to successfully access services tailored to their precise needs. We know that many fail.

When those that are fortunate do manage to access those services, we have an inconsistent approach to quality of the care that we deliver. From maternity services to end of life care and from mental health to primary care, we know that we fail too many of our citizens coming to us, often when they at their most vulnerable. Meanwhile the regulator of care, the Care Quality Commission in England, can do much better in the raising of quality standards. In my opinion, the regulator needs radical change or, at the very least, root and branch review of its inspection-based approach.

We live in an age of rapidly accelerating technological capability whereby there are high expectations for a journey to and from Mars, artificial intelligence and machine learning are talked of by 3-year-olds and your supermarket knows more about you than your spouse, but you are required to endlessly repeat your most basic personal information whenever you access the health service. The disconnect is maddeningly frustrating and requires urgent action, including bold political leadership and vision.

All of the above means that my earlier observation about the service not always being designed based on starting with the patient and working backwards is all too familiar to many. Patients know what they need but they struggle to explain to a health and social care system born in a different age and blessed with structures and pathways of that age. Royal colleges are perfectly worthy and do good work, but their power needs to be more aligned to the yearnings of patients, carers, and bodies, particularly in the voluntary sector, who champion the interests of patients and carers. I might make the same comment about the BMA and RCN. The NHS in each region of the United Kingdom must be allowed to carry out genuine, evidence-based reforms without political interference.

Given all of the resulting uncertainty, frustration and downright angst for patients, it is wonderful that a long standing IHSCM member, Kunle Thomas, has written this book focusing on patients and, specifically, providing practical advice on patient experience.

Many of us in and around the health and social care sector knows that reform and improvement in service design and delivery is much needed - that we can use Kunle's book as a reference point from a patient perspective is all of the encouragement that any of us should need to read and absorb it.

'Start with the patient and work backwards' must be the mantra for anyone involved in NHS quality improvement and redesign. Kunle's book is at least one key for what is a very complex lock.

Jon Wilks
Chief Executive
Institute of Health & Social Care Management (IHSCM)

PREFACE

It has been a journey. A long, slow journey, like on a coach to a distant land. You look out the window and enjoy the beautiful landscapes, cattle and goats grazing on seemingly endless pastures. Then the coach pulls over at a service station for what seems a lifetime. You glance at your watch and wonder how much longer before you get to your destination. The idea of writing this book, and the choice of 'Dear Patient' for the title was conceived a little over 10 years ago! Yes, that long. In 2012, I received a completely unexpected invite to be the keynote speaker at an international patient experience conference in Melbourne, Australia. I was then Head of Patient Experience at East Kent Hospitals University NHS Foundation trust, one of England's largest acute hospital trusts. It turned out that my presentation at a national patient experience conference in London, put together by Health Service Journal (HSJ) a year earlier, played a part. Working for an NHS trust that won the Dr Foster 'Best Hospital trust' award may have come with some unseen perks.

On my return from Australia, I started thinking of how to share my growing knowledge and experience in this specialisation of healthcare management. The seed of writing a book was sown! When the idea of 'Dear Patient' as title came to my mind, I knew I wasn't going to be looking any further. I changed the subtitle a few times before settling for 'A practical guide to patient experience' for its simplicity and encapsulation of my primary objective. Despite enthusiastically starting the research and starting to write the book from about 2013, life got in the way; but the dream was never far from my thoughts.

I quickly realised from my early years of working in the field of patient experience that it wasn't just a job for me – it is my vocation. Having had direct communication with thousands of patients and their families over the years, either as a result of a complaint, a compliment, patient/carer forum activities, and events, I have come to realise that people may hardly remember details of a clinical procedure and the dexterity of the surgeon (assuming a robot was not doing the cutting). What they never forget is the experience - how the nurse or doctor held their hands gently, smiled, and assured them they will be fine. Little things with great impact.

It also dawned on me that should I need medical attention in 20 years' time, the doctors and nurses that will look after me may very well be in primary/elementary schools now. Drugs, instruments, and clinical procedures may have changed by then, but human nature and the need for dignity, empathy and respect will never change. Should AI (artificial intelligence) powered robots increasingly take over the roles of doctors and nurses, how would they in a decade or two show empathy and respect for patients and their carers? The message of patient experience is therefore not just for our doctors, nurses, paramedics and social care professionals of today but also those coming behind in years and decades to come.

It is also my hope that health and social care professionals, not just in the West but in other parts of the globe take patient experience seriously, putting in place all the appropriate structures and systems for checks-and-balances.

To enhance the anonymity of people connected with the cases shared in this book, I have deliberately used regions rather than the actual towns and cities. Even for some of the cases that were well publicised in the media, I have kept to the same principle of enhanced anonymity by not naming the people involved or the city or town where the case originated from.

I sincerely hope readers (or audio book listeners) find *Dear Patient* a useful resource, either as a practitioner, student, or administrator in the health and social care sector. For patients, their carers and families, I hope it provides an empowering knowledge, useful in navigating care services in hospitals and other settings.

Really glad that the dream of writing this book has finally become a reality. What a wonderful coincidence that the book is published in the same month that the 75th anniversary of the National Health Service (NHS) is being celebrated.

Kunle Thomas
July 2023

ACKNOWLEDGEMENT

I would like to express my profound and sincere appreciation to Jon Wilks, the Chief Executive of the Institute of Health and Social Care Management (IHSCM, UK) for taking time out of his very busy schedule to read some material from the book and write the foreword. Jon's foreword is a thought-provoking piece and I encourage every reader of this book to read it.

My heartfelt appreciation also goes to Professor Steve Hams MBE, Chief Nursing Officer; and Dr Jasmine Leonce, Consultant Obstetrician and National Maternity Improvement Adviser. Despite the enormous demand on their time, they both responded positively to my request to read material from the book and provide comments. I feel very humbled and energised by their complimentary remarks.

I am grateful to Dr Arabella Onslow, a GP I am privileged to call a friend, for her support and encouragement when I first came up with the idea of writing the book.

To my daughters, Sabrina and Jessica, I also say thank you for their support and motivation.

There are others, family and close friends, who at different times and places offered me encouragement and support, cheering me on to write and finish the book.

To all of you, I say thank you and God bless.

INTRODUCTION

"Wherever the art of medicine is loved, there is also a love of humanity"

The above quote, over 2400 years old, made by Hippocrates of Cos is proof that patient experience is certainly not a new phenomenon. However, as a dedicated speciality in health care management, patient experience is a relatively new profession.

Patient experience is a specialty dedicated to improving the experience of patients/service users through the critical appraisal of patient and carer feedback it obtains. The experience could relate to any stage of the patient journey, starting from the point of access to aftercare.

Great progress has been made in creating awareness of patient experience and promoting its practice in care settings and among commissioners of health and care services. However, the true appreciation and practice of patient experience is yet to be the norm, even in advanced economies. The days of 'the doctor knows best, so be grateful and be quiet' are almost gone but unfortunately staggers on in some quarters. The key purpose of *Dear Patient – A practical guide to patient experience* is to equip all those working in healthcare - be it as doctors, nurses, paramedics, therapists, administrators or receptionists, and those training or aspiring to these and other health and care roles - with the practical guide to enable them attend to patients, their families and carers with professionalism, courtesy, dignity, and respect. It also provides the public with the knowledge of what is expected of staff in hospitals and other care settings in terms of patient experience, including the handling of complaints and patient/carer engagement. This book uses many real, anonymised cases to illustrate what patient experience is all about, thereby providing a truly practical guide.

The section below looks at the focus of each of the seven chapters.

Chapter 1 Focuses on answering the question: what is patient experience? The answer is not only by way of definition, but also creating a picture of what patient experience would look like in practice. What seems to be the general public understanding of patient experience? Is patient experience about one specific thing or are there different components to it?

Chapter 2 Explores the need for and the process of finding out the experiences of patients. Is the process passive or does it require proactive action? Do you really need to know about the past experiences of patients and carers or is the past best forgotten? If you need to know, how much do you need to know? Would patients be naturally inclined and readily willing to share their experiences? What methodologies and tools could be used for this purpose? Are equality questions avoidable and unnecessary prying, time wasting exercise or a vital 'barometer' for knowing the views of different communities and 'Protected Characteristics'[1] about the health services they receive?

[1] As enshrined in the Equality Act 2010. Designed to protect the rights of communities that are likely to be marginalised. These communities are characterised by factors such as age, ethnicity, faith, disability, sexuality, and gender reassignment.

Chapter 3 looks at the 4 Cs – complaints, concerns, comments, and compliments. It provides a brief description of each 'C' and how they are connected in healthcare delivery. Growing trend of combining PALS[2] and Complaints services into the Patient Experience Department is also explored. Other areas covered in this chapter include the relevance of the 'Duty of Candour'[3] to patient experience and common themes in complaints and concerns. Very importantly, this chapter also provide readers with tips on how healthcare organisations and their staff can increase compliments, reduce complaints, and develop a robust complaints management system.

Chapter 4 reinforces the message that the gathering of patient experience data is not an end in itself but part of a process for achieving positive patient experience. Data collection, triangulation of data from different sources, analysis, interpretation, and reporting are relevant here. Does the data throw up trends and themes? Should the survey report be selectively circulated among staff, or should it be accessible to all staff? Patients' cooperation made the research possible, so should the report be openly available to patients and the public too? What steps should be taken to ensure that poor survey scores are turned around as soon as practically possible?

Chapter 5 focuses on the synergy between patient experience, patient/public engagement and involvement, and communications. Who knows best? Doctors, nurses and other healthcare professionals and administrators on the one hand or patients, their families, carers, and the public on the other? Who knows where the shoe hurts the most? Could that be the person wearing the shoe or the

---

[2] Patient Advice and Liaison Service

[3] Introduced in 2014 as part of the response to the Mid Staffordshire NHS Foundation trust inquiry led by Sir Robert Francis QC

cobbler that makes or repairs the shoe? Could there be any sense in recognising that there is a different but equally relevant 'expertise' in both camps?

This chapter concludes by looking at staff experience and engagement. Charity begins at home, as the old saying suggests. How can staff be made to sing from the same hymn sheet and have the same vision? What is the relevance of the statement: 'happy staff equals happy patients'?

Chapter 6 Why do patients or their families resort to litigation to seek redress? How much is litigation costing the National Health Service (NHS) in England? The fear of litigation has been widely identified as the "evil twin" of litigation – how is this affecting healthcare delivery? Can empathy and accountability in the management of complaints and patient safety incidents influence patients' or their carers/families' propensity to take legal actions against the NHS or indeed any other health care providers? What other measures can help reduce the cost of litigation?

Chapter 7 What challenges did the COVID-19 pandemic pose to health care delivery, particularly from a patient experience perspective? What actions were taken to address the challenges posed. Lastly, what lessons were learned, and still being learned, from the pandemic experience by hospital administrators, including patient experience teams.

CONTENTS

Foreword v
Preface ix
Acknowledgement xiii
Introduction xv

Chapter 1 What is patient experience all about? 1
Chapter 2 The need to know: Data collection, triangulation, and analysis 13
Chapter 3 The Four Cs: Compliments, comments, concerns, and complaints 47
Chapter 4 Using data to improve services: Now that you know, what are you going to do about it? 81
Chapter 5 The synergy effect: Patient experience, patient/public engagement, and communications 91
Chapter 6 Drivers of litigation: The impact of empathy and accountability 119
Chapter 7 Delivering patient experience in a covid pandemic era 137

Bibliography 155

Illustrations and Table

(i) Flowchart: Architectural Framework for Patient Experience...9

(ii) Table of formal & informal complaints involving Doctors/Consultants in a three-month period (Quarter 3: October – December) 69

(iii) Engagement continuum: From making contact to co-production 96

Appendices

Appendix A 2018 National inpatient questionnaire (issued by the Care Quality Commission, England) 165

Appendix B Complaints handling flowchart: Process and time management (Based on a 30-day response time) 177

Appendix C Checklist for investigating a complaint and drafting response letter 178

Appendix D Abbreviations and acronyms commonly used in health and social care and what they mean 182

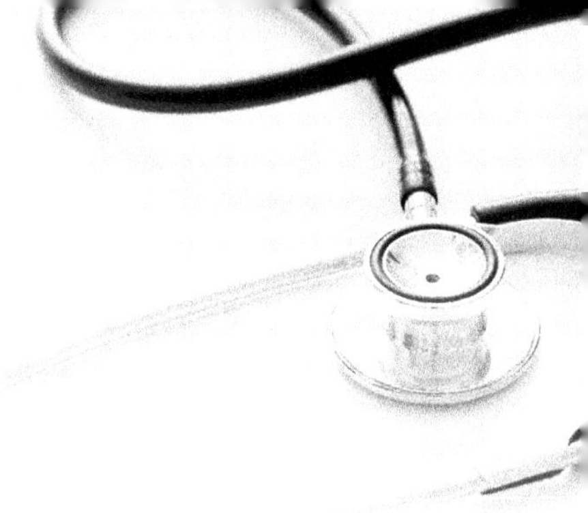

CHAPTER ONE

What is patient experience all about?

This chapter focuses on answering the question: what is patient experience? The answer is not only by way of definition, but also creating a picture of what patient experience should look like in practice. What seems to be the public understanding of patient experience? Is patient experience about one specific thing or are there different components to it?

Patient experience is … well, what is written 'on the tin', the experience of patients! That may be true in the broadest possible sense, but it doesn't really make us any wiser. To throw more light on the subject, two definitions will be provided. The first definition will be an original one by the author, followed by a definition by the Beryl Institute[4]. A patient's true story will then follow, to demonstrate the essence of patient experience. We can then examine the key elements that give patient experience its true meaning.

Patient experience is a science that proactively and responsively focuses on all forms of patient/carer and provider interactions, from the first point of access (online, telephone or physical visit) to after-care support, whilst promoting its hallmarks of dignity, respect, empathy, and professionalism.

The above definition explains why WHO[5] identifies people-centred care as a key component of quality in health care.[6]

The Beryl Institute defines patient experience as:

"The sum of all interactions, shaped by an organization's culture, that influence patient perceptions across the continuum of care."

---

[4] The Beryl Institute describes itself as the "global community of practice committed to elevating the human experience in healthcare." The Institute's head office is based in Nashville, Tennessee, US

[5] World Health Organisation

[6] https://www.who.int/health-topics/quality-of-care#tab=tab_1 (7 October 2022)

CASE STUDY 1:
Patient refuses emergency surgery (London)

The King's Fund[7] shared the experience of an older female patient who was refusing emergency surgery for hip fracture at a London hospital. The patient asked to be discharged back home instead of receiving the urgent care she needed, and in spite of the pain and discomfort she was experiencing. Efforts to make her consent to the surgery proved abortive. It was only after staff took the time to "find out her whole story (beyond the medical questions)"[8] that the rationale for her refusal of emergency surgery became apparent. It emerged that she was carer to her frail husband and didn't want to leave him without adequate support while she received care for herself. It was as if she felt that accepting the emergency treatment would be selfish. Knowing the full story, the hospital was then able to arrange care for the patient's husband while she received surgical treatment for her hip fracture. Killing two birds with a stone, one might say; everyone involved was a winner!

Reflections on the case study

This true story narrated by a doctor who was part of the surgical team looking after the patient paints a real, 'in practice' picture of patient experience – taking time to find out, listening, and then acting with professionalism and empathy.

[7] An independent think tank with a charitable status focused on health and care improvement in England

[8] Dougall, D (2017), 'Listening to patients, carers, staff and communities…do we care enough?' Blog on the website of the King's Fund (accessed 20/08/2021)

- What would have happened if the patient was giving a form to sign for discharging herself? Afterall, she initially insisted on going home without undergoing the procedure, despite her pain and mobility problem.
- How much time could have been spent weighing up patient's right to refuse treatment (as she had mental capacity) versus 'best interest' considerations? Either way, the real issue about the care needs of patient's frail husband would have been missed if not for mixing the simple virtues of patience, listening, and empathy with the team's clinical skills.

Let us examine the distinguishing features of patient experience, as evident in the above definitions and story.

- Proactively seeking information/getting data about the experience of patients and carers and being responsive to feedback.
- Engaging and involving patients and carers in coming up with actions that will improve the patient/carer experience.
- Ensuring that all interactions with patients and carers, either by telephone, website, social media or face-to-face, are done with empathy, dignity, respect, and professionalism.

Proactively seeking information about the experience of patients and carers and being responsive to feedback

A key factor that separates science from other forms of knowledge and disciplines is the use of research. Getting information, ideally primary data, about the interactions of patients and carers regarding health care services is fundamental to understanding what patient experience is all about. Equally important is the responsiveness to feedback. Sources of feedback may include complaints, concerns, comments, compliments, and surveys.

We will return to the subject of data gathering, feedback, and their usage in chapters 2 and 4. For now, suffice to say that gathering information for its own sake is a waste of time and other resources put into it. What matters is that the data is used to understand what the challenges are and then proceeding to develop a plan on how the challenges can be effectively addressed, resulting in service improvement.

Engaging and involving patients and carers in coming up with actions that will improve the patient/carer experience

Getting information about the experiences of patients and carers can only be possible with the cooperation and consent of those patients and carers in sharing their stories or completing a questionnaire. After analysing the data and identifying themes and trends, it is important that patients and carers are again involved in planning for the solutions. If a pair of shoes hurts, no one is better placed in knowing exactly where it hurts than the person that wears the shoes – is a toe or two feeling squeezed or is the pain coming from the back of the foot? There is no doubt that expertise of professionals in health care is vital in understanding the data and developing action plans but having the input of patients and carers will enrich the work and give it a better chance of success.

Ensuring that all interactions with patients and carers, either by telephone, website, social media or face-to-face, are done with empathy, dignity, respect, and professionalism

It is vitally important that those working in healthcare, in both clinical and administrative roles, always remember that the data gathered relates to people, real lives, and not just mere numbers or statements for ward dashboards and board reports. Hence, all interactions with patients and carers should be characterised by empathy, dignity, respect, and professionalism – not on some occasions but every single time. This is the aspect of patient experience that can be seen and felt and often stay in the memory of patients and their families or carers the longest – especially if perceived as very good or very bad. Strange as it may sound to some, most patients and carers tend to remember the way they are spoken to, the warm reassurances or the dismissive wave, the smile or frown, the polite we've-got-your-back tone or the harsh we-know-best tone, long after the clinical care is forgotten. These experiences are what patients and carers are more likely to share with friends and families about the care they receive, and less likely about the clinical interventions.

It is important to stress the role of perception in patient experience. What patients or their carers experience and report may not necessarily be based on fact but on their perception at the time. Clinical and administrative/managerial staff working in the healthcare sector must therefore have it at the back of their minds that they and their organisations will ultimately be judged by perception which may or may not be the actual fact or what was intended. It is therefore as important to be caring, respectful and professional as it is to be seen as being caring, respectful and professional.

CASE STUDY 2:
When glitz doesn't mean great *(London)*

The glitz, modern facilities, and sophistication of hospital buildings does not necessarily equate to the best care, sadly. Conversely, tired-looking old buildings lacking in hi tech should not be written off in the provision of good quality health care. In essence, the message in the saying 'never judge a book by its cover' is well and truly relevant in the provision of care and compassion in any health or social care settings.

This was the point demonstrated in the story of Ms D[9]. The story compared and contrasted Ms D's experience of visiting her mother at a London hospital in an ultra-modern building and her stepfather at another London hospital – old and lacking in some modern facilities. Both patients were admitted for cancer but ironically, the care and compassion received by Ms D's stepfather in the old hospital building was far more celebratory than the 21st century ultra-modern building where her mother was also receiving care for cancer. In fact, Ms D's experience was a total lack of care at the shiny, modern hospital. She summed this up eloquently:

"I would be happy for my nearest and dearest to be treated in the shabby Victorian caverns...but the ... (other hospital) might as well have a sign on its gleaming new façade saying 'Abandon hope all ye who enter here'."

---

9 The Sunday Times, 7 July 2013

Case study reflection

A nice, modern building with all the 'mod cons' is a good thing, but patients and their families should not have to choose between a modern building/facilities and good patient care, with empathy, dignity and respect. The latter is a fundamental requirement and must never be compromised, whether the facilities are ultra-modern or old.

FLOWCHART: ARCHITECTURAL FRAMEWORK FOR PATIENT EXPERIENCE

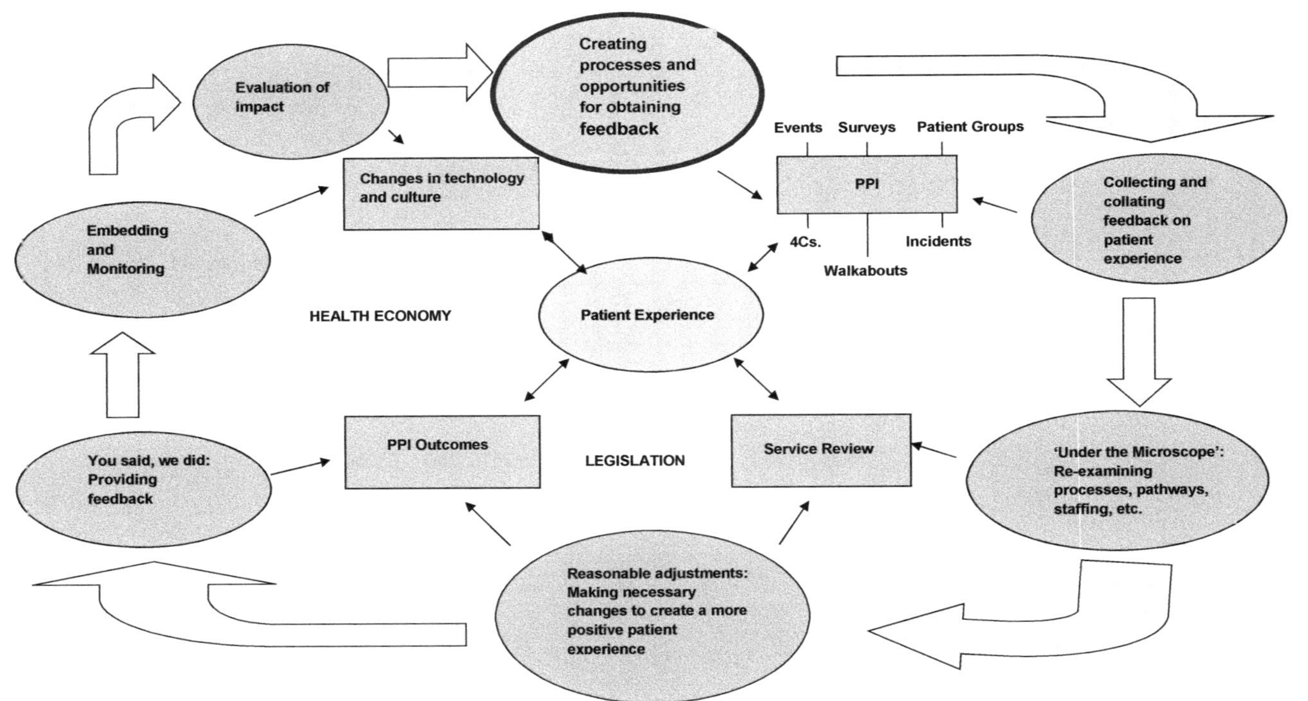

Explanatory notes on the architectural framework for patient experience

Acronyms: PPI (Patient and Public Involvement), 4Cs (Complaints, Concerns, Comments and Compliments)

The diagram shows a cycle of processes and activities that needs to happen as part of a proactive and responsive approach to creating a positive experience for patients, their families and carers.

Collecting and collating feedback using multiple sources, including surveys, walkabouts (internal inspections), and the 4Cs (complaints, concerns, comments and compliments). These are discussed in later chapters.

'Under the Microscope' – Data collected needs to be triangulated and analysed, with the result leading to re-examining processes, pathways, staffing or anything else flagged up by the result. Data collection as an end in itself is a wasted exercise!

Does the data show the need for making 'reasonable adjustments'? If so, act. 'Reasonable adjustment' is a phrase used in the Equality Act 2010 to describe any changes required to improve access, communication and care for patients, carers or staff that are likely to be disadvantaged due to any form of disabilities or any 'protected characteristics'[10]. A clinician or receptionist at a GP[11] practice unable to care and support patients or carers due to a disability should be supported as reasonably as possible by the employer in anticipation

[10] The Equality Act 2010 covers nine 'Protected Characteristics' including age, race/ethnicity, faith, disability, sexual orientation, and gender reassignment.

[11] General Practioner, a primary care doctor

of likely disadvantages or challenges. NICE[12] defines 'reasonable adjustments' as "legal requirement to make sure services are accessible to all people with protected characteristics under the Equality Act."[13]

You said, we did – As the old saying goes, one good turn deserves another. So, when practitioners in health or social care get feedback from patients, carers and other stakeholders, it is only reasonable and fair that they go back with their own updates. It does not mean that all the suggestions must have been implemented before giving updates. It is about demonstrating that they have listened and are transparent about what can be done and what cannot be done because of one reason or the other. Going back with updates builds trust and respect and will go a long way in creating willingness to give feedback in the future.

Embedding and monitoring – Changes and improvements made in service design and delivery needs to be embedded and monitored, to ensure the results are long-lasting and people don't return to the old and familiar. Rewarding and recognising staff and volunteers is one way of achieving this. Others may include regular internal inspections, briefings and training.

Evaluation of impact – If a change is moving progress backwards, perhaps it is time to return to the drawing board for a rethink and redesign, with good patient and carer involvement and ideally co-design. Following the stages in the patient experience flowchart will ensure progress is made. Re-evaluating and monitoring in the face of constant change is important. Changes that are coming our way, especially with advances in technology such as artificial

---

[12] National Institute for Health and Care Excellence

[13] www.nice.org.uk (Accessed 17 June 2022)

intelligence (AI) will be enormous, so we must be ready to reevaluate and adapt if we are to thrive, and not merely survive.

Like most things in life, patient experience does not exist in a vacuum. Changes in legislation, technology, and culture will impact on how we communicate with, listen, and respond to patients, their carers and families. What should always remain constant are the values of empathy, dignity, respect, and professionalism in all interactions with patients and their carers as well as interactions among staff, irrespective of job titles and grades.

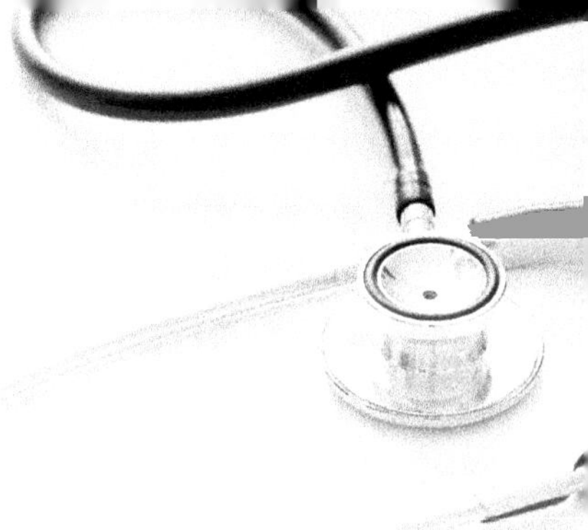

CHAPTER TWO

The need to know: Data collection, triangulation, and analysis

This chapter explores the need for and the process of finding out the experiences of patients. Is the process passive or does it require proactive action? Do you really need to know about the past experiences of patients and carers or is the past best forgotten? If you need to know, how much do you need to know? Would patients be naturally inclined and readily willing to share their experiences? What methodologies and tools could be used for this purpose? Can the 'friends and family test' introduced in the NHS effective 1 April 2013 bring in added value? Are equality questions avoidable and unnecessary prying, or are they a vital barometer for knowing the views of different communities and 'Protected Characteristics'[14] about the health services they receive?

[14] This phrase was coined in the UK Equality Act 2010, with nine 'Protected Characteristics' identified, namely race, age, sex, sexual orientation, disability, gender reassignment, religion or belief, marriage and civil partnership, pregnancy and maternity.

Instinct, gut feeling or 'armchair philosophising'[15] has produced many great successes in different walks of life. In managing patient experience however, instinct should give way to empirical evidence. "I think", "we assume" and speculative deductions cannot be the *modus operandi* if patient experience is to be approached in a methodical, professional, and result-oriented way. This explains the scientific character of patient experience (see author's definition in chapter 1).

To turn a negative patient experience to a positive one, or to make a positive experience even better, there is need to identify what is behind patients' complaint, or what makes them say a big 'thank you'. There is no short cut; ask the question!

But how do you ask the question? Who do you ask, and how many? Where and when do you ask? Each of these questions needs to be carefully considered. Many of those who commission, conduct or use research share the view that research conducted about the same time and focussing on the same issues can have different results depending on how the questions are phrased, whether respondents answer by selecting one or more of a set of fixed options (close ended questions) or they are given the liberty to respond in their own words (open ended questions). Since research is rarely conducted with every single person affected (patients in a GP[16] practice or hospital, students in a school, etc.) being asked questions, how the sample of respondents is chosen and the percentage of the sample in relation to the universal[17] can also skew the result. Research not

[15] Often used to refer to reliance on intuition and own experiences rather than any fact finding or research methodologies.

[16] General Practitioner, family doctor in a primary care setting

[17] The total number of people that are affected by the subject being researched.

using best practice, or in a worst scenario, deliberately fraudulent, can therefore be conducted in ways with a reasonable chance of getting pre-determined results.

In the UK, there are annual national surveys commissioned by the Care Quality Commission (CQC)[18] and focussing on different aspects and sectors of health care. Examples include surveys conducted among inpatients, outpatients, maternity patients, and urgent and emergency care patients. With the support of the service providers such as hospitals, the research company contracted by the CQC contact patients directly. The sample size, conditions of eligibility for inclusion in the sample size, the time of research and other relevant factors are determined by the independent research contractor and same parameters applied across the board. Being a national survey, results for each question are benchmarked, so that each participating healthcare provider can see if they are among the top performers in the country, in the bottom category or squeezed into the middle category. It is not uncommon for an NHS trust to have a high score, say 75%, on a particular question and yet be in the bottom category, as this depends on the scores of the other NHS trusts for that specific question.

National Surveys

National surveys conducted in England started with the adult inpatient survey in 2002. Unlike surveys conducted by individual NHS trusts, national surveys are commissioned by the Care Quality

[18] A non-departmental public body, at 'arm's length' to and funded by the Department of Health and Social Care (DHSC)

Commission (CQC)[19]and the regulatory bodies that preceded it. National surveys are conducted by independent specialist contractors such as Picker.[20]

National adult inpatient surveys

Let us use the 2018 national adult inpatient survey[21] as an example. The 2018 national adult inpatient survey was the country's 16th. 144 acute and specialist NHS trusts took part in the survey. To be eligible to participate in the survey, patients must be at least 16 years of age, had a minimum of one night stay in July 2018. Fieldwork was between August 2018 and January 2019. Fieldwork varied from one NHS trust to another, but the average fieldwork was 14 weeks. A total of 76,000 patients responded to the survey, resulting in a response rate of 45%.

Exclusion criteria were clearly stated, for consistency across the country. These included patients receiving care in the following service areas: obstetrics/maternity, psychiatry, day case (same day discharge), private/non-NHS patients and NHS patients treated at private hospitals. Other exclusions include patients who requested their personal data should be used only for the purpose of their clinical care and patients without a UK postal address.

The survey result was published in June 2019.

---

[19] Care Quality Commission (CQC), established in April 2009 is the independent regulator of health and social care services in England.

[20] Picker Institute Europe

[21] 'NHS Patient Survey Programme. 2018 Adult Inpatient Survey: Quality and Methodology Report'. This was published by the CQC in June 2019

The questionnaire

Scores from a total of 20 questions add up to the Overall Patient Experience Scores (OPES). Though the OPES are no longer in use, in this book they provide a relevant view on how patient experience can be operationalised and measured. The key sections for evaluating the patient experience were:

- Access and waiting (Questions 6, 7, 9)
- Safe, high quality and coordinated care (Questions 33, 50, 60)
- Better information, more choice (Questions 34, 57, 58)
- Building closer relationships (Questions 23, 25,26, 28)
- Clean, friendly, comfortable place to be (Questions 14, 15, 16, 19, 40, 42, 67)

Please see the full questionnaire in Appendix 1.

In a news release[22] on the King's Fund's analysis of 10 years' worth of inpatient survey results, the CQC[23] wrote:

How providers consider and act on patient feedback, including complaints and survey findings, is a core element of our inspections. Where a provider does not have systems in place to do this effectively, this would make us question the quality of its leadership and how 'caring' and 'responsive' its care can be.

Prof Sir Mike Richards
Former Chief Inspector of Hospitals

[22] Published 10/12/2015 and updated 12/05/2022. https://www.cqc.org.uk/news/releases/cqc-welcomes-kings-fund-report-patient-experience-hospitals-over-last-ten-years (Accessed 05/11/22)

[23] Care Quality Commission

Equality questions

The survey identified 11 demographic subgroups, analysed, and compared their experiences of care received. The subgroups included age group, ethnicity, gender, religion, sexual orientation, and long-term health conditions. Other subgroups were respondent (in person or by proxy), case type (medical or surgical), length of stay, ICD-10 chapter code,[24] and route of admission (elective or emergency).

The experiences of the above groups were then compared across themes, namely:

- Information, communication, and education (Questions 30, 36, 56, 63)

  Example: Q30
  Did you know which nurse was in charge of looking after you (this would have been a different person after each shift change)?
  Answer options: 1. Yes, always 2. Yes, sometimes 3. No

- Respect for patient-centred values, preferences and expressed needs (Questions 23, 26, 34, 39, 48)

  Example: Q26
  When you had important questions to ask a nurse, did you get answers that you could understand?

[24] International Classification of Diseases 10th Revision. It is a system used for classifying and coding all diagnoses

Answer options: 1. Yes, always 2. Yes, sometimes, 3. No 4. I had no need to ask

- Emotional support (Questions 37, 38)

  Example: Q37
  Did you find someone on the hospital staff to talk to about your worries and fears?
  Answer options: 1. Yes, definitely 2. Yes, to some extent 3. No 4. I had no worries or fears

- Confidence and trust (Questions 24, 27, 35)

  Example: Q35
  Did you have confidence in the decisions made about your condition or treatment?
  Answer options: 1. Yes, always 2. Yes, sometimes 3. No

- Coordination and integration of care (Questions 32, 54, 61 and 65)

  Example: Q61
  Did hospital staff take your family or home situation into account when planning your discharge?
  Answer options: 1. Yes, completely 2. Yes, to some extent 3. No 4. It was not necessary 5. Don't know/can't remember

- Food choice (Question 20)

  Were you offered a choice of food?
  1. Yes, always 2. Yes, sometimes 3. No

- Hydration (Question 22)

  During your time in hospital, did you get enough to drink?
  Answer options: 1. Yes 2. No, because I did not get enough help to drink
  3. No, because I was not offered enough drinks 4. No, for another reason

- Respect and dignity (Question 67)
  Overall, did you feel you were treated with respect and dignity while you were in the hospital?
  Answer options: 1. Yes, always 2. Yes, sometimes 3. No

Equality and diversity – About You

In the 'About You' section, towards the end of the of the questionnaire, there were eight questions on demographics such as age, gender, ethnicity, religion/faith, disability, and sexual orientation. We will examine the relevance of equality or demographic questions later in this chapter. Why should patients or their carers be asked to complete equality questions in a survey? Are such questions better left out?

Other comments

The last section of the questionnaire, 'Other comments' provided an opportunity to say, in their own words anything they considered important or relevant. There were three questions in this open-ended section:

- Was there anything particularly good about your hospital care?
- Was there anything that could be improved?
- Any other comments?

The 11 sections about the experience of the patients were:

- Admission to hospital
- The Accident and Emergency Department (A&E)[25]
- Waiting list or planned admission
- All types of admission
- The hospital and ward
- Doctors
- Nurses
- Your care and treatment
- Operations and procedures
- Leaving hospital
- Overall

Some of the questions, or indeed sections of the questionnaire, may not be relevant to all patients completing the questionnaire. For example, there were four questions in the Accident and Emergency (A&E) section all of which would not be relevant to patients not admitted to A&E. Similarly, the six questions in the waiting list or planned admission section would be irrelevant to patients admitted through A&E.

---

[25] NHS hospitals in the UK now refer to this as Emergency Department (ED), though A&E remain the popular name for this service/facility among patients and the public

National v Local Surveys

Should health care providers rely solely on annual national surveys, or should they be proactive in conducting local surveys of their own? Let us examine the usual time frame for the national surveys in England.

Fieldwork typically starts around October and ends around January. This is then followed by data analysis and reporting, with the result being published in the summer, about June. Bearing in mind that patients in the sample would have been in the hospital between June and August of the previous year – i.e., up to five months before the commencement of the fieldwork, the gap between the experiences of patients and the publication of the survey findings is typically about a whole year.

Considering the dynamic and fast-paced nature of secondary[26] healthcare delivery, some of the findings may have already been overtaken by new developments. For example, a new catering contractor with a fresh approach to food and nutrition would most likely render obsolete concerns about food quality in a survey conducted almost a year prior.

In addition to the time lag, the national survey result does not give a departmental or ward breakdown, so it is difficult to know where the issues raised emanated from – hence solution cannot be directly targeted at the source of the problem.

It is therefore good practice to conduct local surveys which plug the gaps identified above. Local surveys will also provide proof of

---

[26] Hospital services, as against primary care delivered through GP practices.

consistency, if good scores were achieved in the national survey or prove there has been a turnaround if local survey shows high scores, against poor scores in the national surveys.

Improving survey participation

For most patients, the physical and emotional stress of accessing health services is hard enough. The completion of questionnaires, like other optional tasks, is therefore more likely to be viewed as avoidable burden. So, what can be done to make the completion of questionnaires appealing, or less of a burden, to patients? The following questions should serve as a good check list of factors that can encourage or discourage questionnaire completion.

Does the questionnaire have any identifier? In other words, is there any information to be filled that could make the patient identifiable? This is one of the most significant factors that can encourage or discourage patients from filling a questionnaire. Patients are much more likely to complete a questionnaire if they know it doesn't require them filling their names, addresses, reference numbers of any sort (hospital number, NHS number), etc. Filling a questionnaire should be seen as a free and open space to write what they wish to write about their experiences and perceptions without the fear that the Sword of Damocles[27] may soon be swinging over their head!

Is the questionnaire as short as it could possibly be? The shorter and easier to fill a questionnaire is, the more willing patients or their

[27] Legend or myth in which the servant Damocles swapped places with his master Dionysius II of Syracuse but begged to return to being a courtier because of the 'sword' hanging over him.

carers would be to complete it. It is far better to get 100 patients to fill in a one-page questionnaire made up of the key relevant questions than to get 10 patients to fill in a five-page questionnaire with the questions having varying degrees of relevance.

Does the questionnaire spell out its purpose right from the start? A brief, succinct statement why the survey is being conducted is important and would likely make a big difference to the response rate. Questionnaires aiming to use feedback to improve services or get a better understanding of patients' preferences (e.g., clinic opening times) usually draws on the patients' sense of duty and citizenship.

Are the questions and answer options clear and wording simple and jargon free? It is best practice to test the questionnaire in patient groups or even among young children. Patients shouldn't have to need a dictionary or turn to google search engine to understand the questions or answer options.

When is a question not a question? When it has more than one question! It is important to avoid packing two or more questions in one, as this is certain to confuse patients and their carers. Two for the price of one is great bargain in the shops but the concept is usually not helpful in questionnaire design.

Is there a box for patients to write their comment, in their own words? Whilst a questionnaire might be mainly close ended,[28] having at least one box for 'In your own words…..', 'Any other comment' or something to that effect is very useful as it provides patients the opportunity to say what they really would like to say about the service. Not having this opportunity may put off some patients or deny

[28] Questions can only be answered by ticking one or more boxes of possible answers

the researcher of rich qualitative data. Comments from this source, if positive, are usually quoted by organisations as proof of positive patient experience.

Questionnaire completed but how does it get to the right team?

This salient question brings to mind a classic quote "Breakfast was over, and none had breakfasted"[29] (Bronte, 1847). Getting a lot of patients filling a questionnaire is only half the picture. The other issue is – how do you ensure the completed questionnaire gets to the right team or place for collation and analysis. Some may fill in a questionnaire and not bother to submit it if they have to provide an envelope and/or a stamp for postage themselves. The more options and ease of submitting the completed questionnaire, the better.

The provision of comment boxes in strategic locations such as the lobby, wards, clinic waiting rooms, near PALS[30] office would make it easy for patients to complete the form and drop it in a comment box anonymously and without delay.

Consideration must be given to patients who may not have the time, perhaps not feeling well enough or not in the right frame of mind to complete the questionnaire while at the clinic or hospital. To encourage submission if they have to take it home, the provision of envelope and freepost facility could make a huge difference to the response rate.

---

[29] From Jane Eyre, the bildungsroman-cum-gothic 19th century novel by Charlotte Bronte

[30] Patient Advice and Liaison Service

Don't forget electronic option

If you won't put all your eggs in one basket, then don't make your questionnaire available only in paper form! There is no doubt that computer and internet technology has revolutionised every facet of communication, including all forms of giving feedback about services or goods. This could be a simple Word document that can be sent as e-mail attachment or as a form that can be accessed via websites or social media platforms such as Facebook, Twitter or YouTube.

There is a fast-growing sector specialising in providing an array of platforms and tools for obtaining patient feedback electronically – be it on small hand-held electronic devices or electronic kiosks providing additional services such as searching and printing of patient information leaflets.

Health care providers and commissioners should however know what they are trying to achieve and the electronic tools that can help deliver that in a simple and cost-efficient way.

Friends and Family Test (FFT)

On 25 May 2012, David Cameron, then the Prime Minister of UK announced the plan to add the Friends and Family Test to the armoury of survey tools in NHS England. Commenting on the plan to make the FFT results public, the then Prime Minister said in his speech:

"Publishing the answers will allow the public to compare healthcare services and clearly identify the best performers in the eyes of patients - and drive others to take steps to raise their standards...By making those answers public we're going to give everyone a really clear idea of where to get the best care – and drive other hospitals to raise their game."[31] (Department of Health and Social Care, 2012)

Effective April 2013, FFT was introduced as additional tool for assessing England's healthcare delivery in hospitals. Based on the concept of 'Net Promoter Score'[32], the FFT is a simple, standardised survey for finding out the perception of patients about the hospital services received. It is generally believed that people are protective of their family and close friends, and so if they can be confident enough to recommend the health care services received to their family and friends, it must be good enough to deserve such recommendation, hence Friends and Family Test.

---

[31] News release from the Department of Health and Social Care, 25 May 2012: 'Friends and Family' test aims to improve patient care and identify best performing hospitals

[32] Customer loyalty metric introduced by Fred Reichheld in his 2003 Harvard Business Review article "One Number you need to Grow."

The FFT was first introduced in hospital wards and in Emergency Department (ED)[33] and in October 2013 it was extended to cover NHS funded maternity services. NHS staff followed in April 2014. The FFT survey has gone through various changes, including the introduction of the comment section, allowing open-ended response. As noted above, in the last paragraph of the section on 'Improving survey participation', the use of open-ended, comment section is a great incentive that allows respondents to give feedback in their own words, about what really matters to them. This could be positive, negative or neutral for the service provider and should help them to provide targeted improvement.

It is also worth adding that FFT is now widely used in the NHS and NHS funded hospitals, GP surgeries, dental practices, mental health services, community care, emergency department/A&E as well as patient transport service.

The Question

If on a ward

"How likely are you to recommend our ward to friends and family if they needed similar care or treatment?

If in Emergency Department (A&E)

"How likely are you to recommend our A&E department to friends and family if they needed similar care or treatment?"

[33] Originally known as Accident and Emergency (A&E)

The Response

There are six possible responses, ranging from 'extremely likely' to 'extremely unlikely', with two of the six responses being neutral, non-judgemental ('neither likely nor unlikely' and 'don't know').

The scale below should be used to answer the question:

1 ☐ Extremely likely

2 ☐ Likely

3 ☐ Neither likely nor unlikely

4 ☐ Unlikely

5 ☐ Extremely unlikely

6 ☐ Don't know

Criticisms of the original form of Friends and Family Test (FFT)

The introduction of the FFT in its original form divided healthcare professionals and research experts as to its value. Some argue that the original version of the FFT was flawed; reasons include the following:

- One question cannot provide adequate opportunity for patients to express how they truly perceive the service

- Researchers studying patients and public responses to and understanding of the Friends and Family Test found that many patients were confused as to what they were meant to 'recommend'. They described the FFT in its original form as not conforming to basic scientific standards which failed to measure up to the 'lofty declarations' in the FFT's implementation guidance. (Reeves, 2013).

New change from 1 April 2020

The original question of asking patients if they would recommend the service received to friends and family has now changed, replaced by a question seeking to gauge patient's overall experience and level of satisfaction. Considering that this latest change was introduced as the country was coming to terms with the Coronavirus (COVID-19) pandemic and battling to contain it, getting health care providers to brief their staff on the implications of the change was unlikely to be a priority whilst dealing with a pandemic.

CASE STUDY 3: A close look at comments from Friends and Family Test (FFT) *(London)*

FFT comments made over a three-month period were reviewed so as to better understand the picture of patient experience and therefore be able to pinpoint aspects of the hospital service that required improvement or worthy of sharing as best practice.

The FFT comments reviewed were from the inpatient and emergency department results for Quarter 4 (Jan – March). For the inpatients, the total number of responses was 834. The percentage of sample size used was 100%, with every single respondent writing in the comment column. Fully complimentary/positive comments accounted for 74.3% (620) while fully negative comments accounted for only 7.8% (65). 12.1% (101) patients provided positive comments with a 'but', adding negative comments to their feedback. 5.7% (48) of respondents gave comments that were neither positive nor negative, categorised as neutral – these included 2 'no comments'.

A total of 3,841 patients responded to the Emergency Department (ED/A&E) FFT survey. Due to the large number, random sampling was used to select a sample size of 33.4% (1285).

Examples of compliments for in-patient wards

- The best!
- Family-like care, warm and friendly
- Going the 'extra mile', nothing too much – in spite of being very busy
- Good clinical care
- Very professional

Examples of concerns for in-patient wards

- Long wait for most services (clinical care, test results, response to ward buzzer, discharge, transport, medication, etc.) – most recurring concern, by far
- Poor discharge process, including medication and staff attitude

- Low staffing level – causing long wait
- Night shift team "a bit too casual", in contrast to very helpful day staff. "Night staff had more sleep than patients", "I didn't feel safe with the night staff"
- Noisy; prevented sleep at night. Also noisy in the morning during handover

Compliments for Emergency Department/A&E

- Professional, in spite of the pressure staff were under
- Courteous and friendly
- Confident
- Quick ("I was treated promptly…it only took 1½ hours in total despite being packed. I was thrilled", "The service was quick and everything was fine") – suggesting the theme of long waiting time is not a consistent problem

Concerns for Emergency Department/A&E

- Long waiting time – to be seen by doctor, to get medication etc
    - "The waiting time is ridiculous. I had to wait 8 hours before seeing a doctor"
    - "I was satisfied with the treatment. I was not satisfied with the waiting"

  Putting the waiting time issue in perspective, patients commented:
    - "I was looked after very well, but I did have to wait a long time as there was a lot of people to be seen. That wasn't their fault, however"

- "...I had to wait long time but that is no one's fault, afterwards the treatment was excellent"
- Understaffing – opined to be partly responsible for the long waits
  - One patient summed this up: "There was a long wait... Its such a big department with hardly any staff...You need more staff."
  - Another said: "I had a very long wait....It needs more staffing"
- Communication gap – between staff and patients, between services and departments
  - "There needs to be communication as to waiting time as we are humans"
  - Staff wouldn't speak to me and cut me dead. Awful experience"
- Staff attitude
  - "The nurse that I saw was extremely rude...Even my partner was taken aback by how rude the nurse was."
  - "A doctor told me to shut up"
- Handover and how well joined up
  - "...night team forgot to follow up my case"

Case study reflections

Comments often appear clustered. For example, one batch of responses were overwhelmingly complimentary while the next batch were mostly negative. The clustered comments often relate to duration of visit and attitude of staff at the time.

Long waiting time was an issue in both inpatient wards and AE/ED, and so was staffing problem. In what ways would adequate staffing impact quality of care, patient experience, and staff experience?

Equality questions

Why include in a survey equality questions such as those relating to age, gender, ethnic origin, faith, disability, and sexuality?

Work experience in healthcare has shown that in most cases, the inclusion of equality questions in surveys is not consistent. If anything, it would be missed out in most cases if left in the hands of doctors, nurses and other allied health professionals. Managers, if not under the watchful gaze of the Equality and Diversity Manager (or any other similar role) may do better than their clinical counterparts but still come short. Most tend to see the inclusion of equality questions as unnecessary 'bolt on' that needs to be there in order to avoid one form of sanction or the other.

Let us start from the perspective of staff. Why do most people working in the healthcare sector fail to include equality questions in their surveys? The answers often vary and include the following:

- Don't think it is necessary
- Makes the survey much longer than necessary
- Patients don't want to be asked such questions anyway
- I wouldn't like to share such information myself
- What difference does that make to the care they need?

But what do patients themselves think about equality questions? To answer this, let us turn to the case study below.

CASE STUDY 4:
Equality questions: Threat or opportunity?
(South East England)

At a patient and public engagement event held by an NHS hospital trust in Southeast England, one of the topics discussed by patients/carers, representatives of the voluntary sector and staff was the inclusion of equality questions in questionnaires. To kick off the discussion, the hospital staff presented a paper 'Help us to help you better – why we need to collect equality data'. This introduction to the debate clearly made a case for the inclusion of equality questions in questionnaire. The key points include:

- Statutory requirement for providers and commissioners of health services to know the different 'Protected Characteristics'[34] that use their services, to enable staff support patients better
- To make members of such groups and communities feel valued by showing the willingness to listen to their specific needs and issues
- To create awareness among staff and the wider community of the needs of these groups and thereby root out the myths

[34] Phrase introduced in the Equality Act 2010 to describe factors that tends to make some groups of people more likely to be discriminated against or treated less fairly than other groups. These factors are race, gender, age, disability, sexuality and faith. Others added in the 2010 Act are gender reassignment, civil partnership/marriage and pregnancy/maternity.

and fabrications upon which discrimination and unfair treatment may thrive.

Despite the above introduction to the debate, over 75% of those attending disagreed with the need to ask equality questions. Their views can be summarised as follows:

- Irrelevant to health needs
- Amounts to invasion of privacy
- Waste of time; simply don't answer them
- Very annoying to be asked such questions

The few positive or neutral comments include:

- Don't mind, if used to improve services for every group
- You don't have to put your name or any contact details, so it's fine by me
- Important to give people choice to complete or not – must not be compulsory.

Case study reflections

Most patients are very sensitive about their personal data, especially those relating to their sexuality, faith, disability, and other 'Protected Characteristics'. The onus is therefore on health and care professionals to approach the subject with sensitivity and full understanding of the arguments for and against such disclosures. To get the cooperation of patients for this purpose, setting out the purpose of that data collection is as vital as to the tone and sensitivity applied in approaching the subject.

Other sources of data on patient experience

Apart from the use of different forms of surveys, what other tools and processes can be used to collect data on patient experience? These include:

- Compliments, comments, concerns and complaints (the 4Cs)
- Claims
- Patient safety incidents
- Patient stories
- Patient group/forum meetings
- Events
- Focus group
- Walkabouts
- Mystery shoppers

Compliments, comments, concerns and complaints (the 4Cs) – let us skip this at this point as it is the focus of attention in chapter 3

Claims

Patients or their families and carers can make a claim against an NHS trust or any other provider if they feel they have been harmed by the treatment they received (or should have received) or they have incurred avoidable expenses or financial loss due to the way their care was managed. Their rationale for making a claim is not only relevant for determining the merit of their claim but also an insight into their experience and lessons to be learned.

Patient safety incidents

When things go wrong, or could have gone wrong, in the process of delivering care in hospitals or other health care settings, these are described as patient safety incidents. To understand what happened, how and why in order to avoid a repeat of such incidents, an investigation is conducted. The framework for such investigations is known as the Serious Incident (SI) Framework. A major change is happening in the NHS, as the SI Framework is being replaced by the Patient Safety Incident Response Framework (PSIRF). PSIRF is expected to replace the SI Framework by the Autumn of 2023.

Patient stories

The use of patient stories as a barometer for measuring patient experience is well established but unfortunately not yet standard practice. This is a powerful tool that captures the confidence, relief, fears, anxieties, and other such emotions that quantitative surveys cannot capture.

The patient story could be obtained through interviews and documented on paper, audio, or video. The patient or carer can also relay their story in person. Many NHS trusts in England, and most likely across the UK, now include it in their agenda at some of their board meetings. Some NHS trusts feature a patient story at every board meeting, some at every other board meeting whilst others are yet to embrace this powerful tool. Worth adding that patient stories should not be shared exclusively with the board. Different staff groups can also benefit, including frontline staff such as Health Care Assistants

(HCAs), nurses, doctors, ward managers, ward receptionists, and matrons.

Consent

It is important to stress that every patient or carer sharing their story must be told how and where the recorded material would be used and must be made to sign a consent form that they are happy for their story to be used as such. As with any type of consent, the purpose, usage and media must be clearly explained, and the patient/carer given the opportunity to withdraw consent within a specified period of time. In other words, it should never be a 'one sitting process' whereby the explanation (i.e., why the recorded patient story is important, how and where the recorded material will be used, etc.) is given and immediately a form is produced for the patient to sign with no option of opting out afterwards.

Getting best value from patient stories

As noted above, it is recommended that the story is recorded – most ideally a video recording, if possible. Once recorded, how can it be put to the most effective use? It is helpful to gauge the knowledge and experience of the audience before sharing the recorded material. This could be done by a brief talk on the subject before or during the playing of the video, followed by audience comments. It could also be preceded by a question-and-answer session. The session could then end with another brief talk, relating the patient story with comments made prior to the sharing of the recording, and highlighting lessons to bear in mind for the future.

Key messages from the patient story and lessons learned should be agreed and cascaded to all staff.

Feedback at patient group meetings

Patient groups are vital for effective communication between healthcare organisations (hospitals, GP practices, etc.) on one hand and patients and the wider public on the other. If set up with a genuine purpose of providing feedback on patient experience, then the membership should, at least to some extent, reflect the diversity in the patient population. The members should not be self-serving but act as a conduit through which patient and public feedback is shared with the healthcare organisation and information from health and care providers is shared with the patient population, families and carers.

In addition to passing information from the healthcare organisation to patients, patient groups should have a real opportunity to shape and influence policies, strategies, and decisions.

The frequency and mode of meetings among patient groups vary. However, most tend to meet monthly, bi-monthly, or quarterly. Feedback from patient groups may be in various forms and from various sources including:

- Experiences of group members, friends, family, and neighbours who used, or are using services as patients or carers

- Questionnaires and interviews
- Intelligence on a specific issue – gathered from patients and/or the local communities

It is vitally important for health and care providers to respond within a reasonable or agreed timeframe to the feedback from patient forums: You said, We did; couldn't do because of one reason or another.

Responding to feedback provided is like the oil that keeps the machine running smoothly. It shows respect for the patient representatives who are members of the forums, and by extension to the wider patient population and local communities that the forums represent. It is also a demonstration and acknowledgement that the work of the patient forums is important to quality improvement in the relevant care settings.

Events

Events are a great source of obtaining feedback from patients and the public. Events often combine the social, relaxation and entertainment aspects with the business aspect – discussions, sub-group exercises and stalls/exhibitions. While the main attraction for some may be the discussion and feedback session, for others the attraction may be the social interactions and networking; there is often something for everyone.

CASE STUDY 5:
It's good to prompt, especially if issue is 'private and personal' *(South East England)*

'How come there was no mention of pain during sex?' It was a 76-year-old woman posing the question after a presentation on therapy services available at an NHS hospital. It was a public event organised to attract new members for the hospital Foundation trust[35] and to raise awareness on a common health condition, on this occasion, pain.

A few other members of the public present then spoke in support of the point raised, stressing that nurses, doctors, and allied health practitioners should make it easier for patients and their carers to talk about intimate subjects by providing prompts. By asking the question or including such information in patient information leaflets, presentation materials and websites, patients and carers may feel more confident in seeking help for such conditions. It may be misguided to expect patients and carers to talk about any intimate health issues affecting them, such as those relating to sex, without recognising that some people may never seek help for health conditions they consider 'off limits' if not given a gentle nudge of approval to do so.

The hospital staff were very appreciative of this point and promised to take it on board.

[35] Foundations trusts form a big part of the National Health Service (NHS) in England. They have more discretion in the way they manage their affairs (compared to NHS trusts without the Foundation trust status), using their membership and governors for an extra layer of governance.

Case study reflections

It is never just about what is being said but equally important is how it is being communicated – the approach and tone of delivery.

Apart from sex, what other issues tend to be treated as very personal and not openly discussed? For many, faith is another good example. Sexuality?

The more open patients and carers become in voicing any concerns in health and care settings, the quicker their access to factual advice and support. There is a duty of care on the part of staff to be non-judgemental, empathetic and supportive.

Focus Group

Focus groups is another source of patient experience. Unlike a patient group, a focus group tends to focus on a particular issue or subject rather than a general, ongoing subject. In other words, focus groups are usually ad-hoc by nature. They are characterised by:

- Focus on a subject or issue
- Ad-hoc
- Main activity is discussion
- Mostly generates qualitative data

Powell and Single (1996)[36] defines a focus group as "a group of individuals selected and assembled by researchers to discuss and

[36] Powell, R A and Single, H M (1996)

comment on, from personal experience, the topic that is the subject of the research." Powell and Single traced the origin of this research method to the 1920s.

Focus groups may be ideal in 'feeling the pulse' of the patient population on issues such as hospital food, discharge, and GPs out-of-hours service. There is hardly any subject relevant to the experience of patients that a focus group cannot be used to explore.

Organisations using focus groups should be mindful of its composition, and the potential of a vocal few drowning out the views of others – hence the moderator's role is very significant.

Walkabouts (Internal inspections)

As the name suggests, walkabouts refer to a small group of people - usually a mix of staff (clinical/managerial), board and patients – who walk round the premises and facilities to see first-hand how patients are being cared for and treated. This may involve talking to patients about their experience of the service as well as talking to staff. Apart from observing staff at work and talking to patients, it allows for inspection of equipment and facilities, especially as a faulty equipment may not only give rise to appalling patient experience but can cause injury or death.

Walkabouts as a source of patient experience is critically important as it provides data in real time, as things unfold as against reading a report about them later.

Mystery shoppers

This is a useful source of patient experience data, though a controversial one in terms of ethics. Like walkabouts, mystery shoppers gather data about patient experience as they happen. However, while the former is visible and usually pre-announced, mystery shoppers – as the name suggests – are like flies on the wall, with their ears to the ground.

Mystery shoppers play the role of detectives, so they are able to gather information without the observed knowing they are being observed. Mystery shoppers eliminates the possibility of 'playing to the camera' whereby patients or staff may behave in certain ways or say certain things simply because they know some officials are there to observe and make notes.

This source of patient experience data has divided both the healthcare professionals and patients due to ethical considerations. Some argue that it is most unfair to snoop around in order to gather information while others believe that it provides a source of unadulterated data as people would be recorded doing what they would naturally do rather than what they would do if aware they are being observed. The latter group argue that the media widely use this method of data collection in their tell-all documentaries, hence better for the organisation to use the same tactics and address the revelations internally rather than being exposed by the media in this way. This ethical consideration therefore takes us back to the age-old question: does the end justify the means?

In October 2012, Panorama programme by BBC1[37] broadcast a damning report about the care of vulnerable patients at Winterbourne View Care Home. The broadcast was based on the evidence obtained by an undercover reporter who posed as a Care Worker. Six staff were jailed as a result of the evidence for "institutional abuse". Castlebeck, owners of Winterbourne View apologised for the abuse and suspended 13 staff.

[37] A channel of the British Broadcasting Corporation

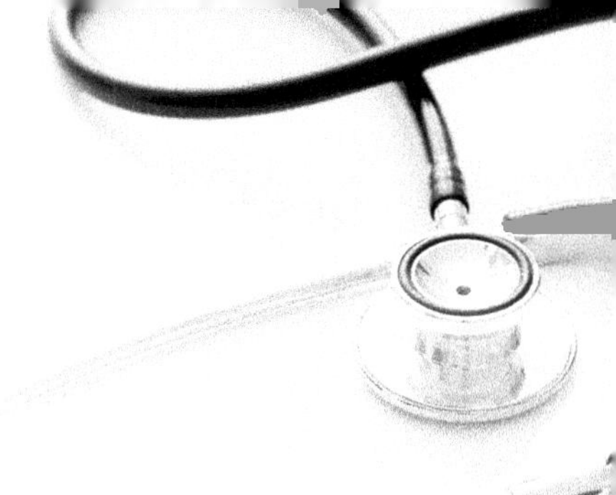

CHAPTER THREE

The Four Cs: Compliments, comments, concerns, and complaints

Brief description of each 'C' and how they are connected in healthcare delivery. Is the Patient Experience Department of a health care organisation just about the management of complaints and PALS (Patient Advice and Liaison Service)? Relevance of the 'Duty of Candour' to patient experience. Common themes in complaints and concerns. Tips on how to increase compliments, reduce complaints, and develop a robust complaints management system.

The findings of my investigations reveal an attitude – both personal and institutional – which fails to recognise the humanity and individuality of the people concerned and to respond to them with sensitivity, compassion and professionalism.[38]

Ann Abraham
Parliamentary and Health Service Ombudsman for England
(November 2002 – December 2011)

I'm sorry I can't help you; it's not my job. If you wish to complain, take one of the 'How to Complain' leaflets or go and see the complaints team or PALS on the ground floor. This was the comment, paraphrased, made by a member of staff of an NHS trust in response to a patient's concern.

It is common for staff in the health sector to tell patients something similar to the above statement. Irrespective of the circumstances, is this the right response from staff to an aggrieved patient or carer? Absolutely NOT. The author's analogy on this subject is that of a table tennis/ping pong ball being deflected only for the individual to end up with a head-on collision with a golf ball! Both balls are often white, round and small but with a massive difference in their weight and therefore impact they would make if they hit someone. Trying to avoid dealing with the concern of a patient or carer/family at the first opportunity is what the author likens to deflecting a table tennis ball. The complaint usually does not go away but gather momentum. The increased momentum in the form of a formal complaint is what is likened in this analogy to a head-on collision with a golf ball!

---

[38] From the report: 'Care and compassion? Report of the Health Service Ombudsman on ten investigations into NHS care of older people'. Published February 2011.

Of the 4 Cs, complaint is the one you get to hear about the most – both among staff and in the media. It brings to mind bands of musicians or performing artists where one of the members towers above the rest in terms of popularity or notoriety.

It is worth stressing that though we tend to hear more about complaints, most healthcare providers record many more compliments than complaints. Some trusts have their volume of compliments double the volume of complaints and some have a ratio 1:20 or more, so the spectrum is wide.

There is a public perception that more complaints mean the service must be worse in comparison with service provider with less complaints. Surprisingly, this is often not the case.

Healthcare organisations that make it easy for patients/carers to complain, including promotion of the access and process of making complaints, are more likely to obtain feedback that could help improve the quality of their services, provided the feedback are acted upon. Conversely, providers that do the barest minimum to promote access to their complaint process may get far less complaints and, on the surface may look better than the provider with more complaints simply because they actively promote access to their complaint process. The vital point to note is that unreported concerns are like dirt swept under the carpet whilst providers that promote access to their complaints process can be likened to a scenario where carpets are rolled up and furniture moved to allow access to the dirt and dust, hence able to keep the room 'spick and span'[39]. The clean room in the analogy would mean safer care and enhanced patient experience.

[39] Very clean

Let us now turn our attention to a brief description of each of the 4 Cs and examine how they are connected in healthcare delivery.

Compliments

The author has chosen to start with compliments, with the hope it can regain its lead position in the minds of patients, public and healthcare staff.

Compliments, as the name suggests, simply refers to the 'thank you' messages received by health and care providers – be it a GP practice or hospital of any variety.

It is important for organisations to bear in mind that a compliment does not simply mean a 'thank you' letter received from a patient, their carer or family. While that is a key part of it, other ways used in saying 'thank you' must also be considered. These may include – 'thank you' cards, flowers, 'thank you' telephone calls, e-mails, text messages, twitter and Facebook messages or physical drop ins where a team or staff is visited for the purpose of expressing appreciation.

There are also many occasions when patients or their carers/families bring in or send gifts such as cakes and chocolates. In some cases, they send cheques, often as a donation to a specific service or to support the work of the health care organisation's charity. For providers to get a true account of the compliments they receive, they must develop a system that tracks all the different ways patients and their loved ones use in conveying their appreciation of the service whilst also monitoring the different offices or teams where the compliments may be sent. Latter may include the PALS[40] team, Chief Executive's office, wards, and Consultants' Personal Assistants.

CASE STUDY 6: Spotting the hidden compliments *(South East England)*

Over 100% increase was recorded in the compliments for the fourth quarter report at an NHS hospital trust in South East England, compared with compliments for quarter 1 in the same financial year. This impressive increase was not simply due to more patients, their families and carers complimenting the trust for its services. A significant proportion of the increase was in fact due to spotting the hidden compliments.

A system was put in place whereby every ward and every department would forward compliments received every month to a central source where the data was collated and analysed. All wards and departments were briefed that the compliments must not be limited to letters, but all the other sources identified above such as flowers, 'thank you' cards and verbal compliments. Only the data is required. Surely, the chocolate would have long gone!

Case study reflections

A few decades ago, most information coming through the intercom on the London Underground related to travel disruptions and delays.

[40] Patient Advice and Liaison Service

Fast forward to recent times, London Underground regularly compliments itself by telling passengers about all the lines that are running smoothly. And why not? NHS hospitals gather compliments and share good practice but much more can be done in celebrating compliments and the staff that earned them whilst continuing to address issues raised through complaints.

Comments

This is perhaps the least known and least recorded of the 4 Cs. Comments refers to views and ideas of patients, their carers, families, or visitors. This could be borne out of their experience of the service or informed by their knowledge or other experiences. Many researchers suggest that healthcare is one of the things people are most concerned about in life, hence not surprising that people are willing to share their ideas and views of how the healthcare system or specific health care services can be improved upon. In the UK, the NHS is one of the most loved and cherished institutions. Remember the opening ceremony of the London Olympics in 2012? The ceremony displayed a befitting tribute to the NHS and a demonstration of the public's adulation for this iconic British institution.

It is imperative that healthcare organisations log comments received and respond with their own 'thank you' message in acknowledgement of the time and effort taken to write and send the comments.

Concerns

Concerns refer to informal complaints or flagging of things that may go wrong. It may also be about things that went wrong but not deemed serious enough by PALS[41] or the patient to warrant a formal complaint. Common examples may relate to parking problems, attitude of staff, delayed or cancelled appointments or may relate to an inpatient's food portion being too small or hot food served cold.

Experience of working in the NHS shows that many hospital trusts don't pay enough attention to concerns, devoting instead almost all of their resources for patient experience to the management of complaints.

One of the key messages of this book is that organisations that pay significant attention to concerns will not only have fewer complaints, and therefore more time being spent on actual patient care but will in addition engage better with their patient population. Such organisations are also more likely to record higher levels of patient satisfaction than organisations that pay little or no attention to managing concerns.

Organisations should bear in mind the table tennis ball and golf ball analogy used above, as patients/carers are at liberty to escalate their PALS concerns to formal complaints.

Complaints

Complaints are formal expressions of grievances. They are often presented in writing (on paper, by e-mail or via digital platforms) and

[41] Ditto

tends to deal with serious allegations or concerns. Usually, complaint letters are addressed to the Chief Executive of the organisation. However, letters addressed to the Head of Complaints Department, the Ward Manager or manager responsible for the service in question should not get less attention.

Of all the 4 Cs, complaints have the most formalised process:

- They have to be acknowledged within a reasonably short period of time, usually within two or three working days. A growing trend is to prepare a detailed acknowledgement letter that is sent out automatically when an email is received in the complaints inbox. The auto-response can only be generic and used for complaints received by email only, hence those received by post and through other sources must be acknowledged manually. The main benefits of the auto-response are to help boost the overall percentage of complaints acknowledged within the number of days specified in the organisation's complaints policy and to reassure the complainant that their complaint has been received and being dealt with. At the acknowledgement stage, the organisation must set a timeframe for processing the complaint and sending a response. The timeframe should not be set in stone, making it clear that circumstances may cause a response delay. Should that happen, the complainant must be advised well in advance of the original response due date, with an explanation of why the response is being delayed and when the response can be expected. This should ideally be a two-way communication and negotiation.
- The response letter, addressing all the issues raised must be in line with the agreed timescale. Prior to 1 April 2009, 25

working days (essentially five weeks, minus weekends and bank/public holidays) was the maximum time allowed for this phase. Many NHS trusts now have two or three deadlines, depending on the complexity of the complaint. The minimum response time still hovers around 25 – 30 working days, with some NHS trusts proposing between 45 – 60 days for the resolution of complex complaints at the local/trust level.

- If not resolved at the local resolution stage, the complainant can refer the complaint to the Parliamentary and Health Service Ombudsman (PHSO) if they so wish. This information, including contact details for the PHSO must be communicated to the complainant by the NHS trust concerned, giving the patient the choice of escalating the complaint.
- The independence of the PHSO[42] is designed to give patients/carers who wish to escalate their complaints the added reassurance of impartiality and fairness. This is often the final stage of the complaints process, though complaints may be further escalated to judicial review in exceptional cases.

A 'best practice' in patient experience is recording and learning from both PALS[43] concerns and complaints, not just complaints. Healthcare organisations that take concerns as seriously as they do complaints are almost certain to end up with fewer complaints and their patients having more positive experience. Also, most patients or carers will escalate their concerns to formal complaints if they are not taken seriously.

[42] Parliamentary and Health Service Ombudsman

[43] Patient Advice and Liaison Service

CASE STUDY 7: Hospital misdiagnosed breast cancer[44] *(East of England)*

Ms X, aged 40 attended an appointment at the hospital's breast clinic in February 2010, having been referred as urgent by her GP[45]. Ms X reported pain, swelling, and some hardness in her left breast around the areola.[46]Doctor A asked for an ultrasound scan to be done and diagnosed Ms X with mastitis[47]. Doctor A prescribed antibiotics and arranged a follow up appointment for Ms X in three weeks' time. Unfortunately, Ms X was unable to attend this appointment, so a new follow up appointment was arranged for May 2010. At this appointment, a new doctor, Doctor B attended to Ms X. Despite noticing a new 'spot' that was not visible at the appointment with Dr A, in addition to the thickening of the skin in the areola,[48] no test was performed, and a follow up appointment was scheduled for August 2010 i.e., three months' time. DNA[49] was recorded for the August appointment, resulting in Ms X being discharged from the service.

It was 14 months since Ms X was discharged before a new GP referral was received, and Ms X was again seen at the breast clinic in December 2011. At this appointment, patient had an ultrasound scan and a mammography[50] which showed a 9cm mass in Ms X's

[44] Report by the Parliamentary and Health Service Ombudsman (2014)

[45] General Practitioner (primary care doctor)

[46] Area of darker skin around the nipple

[47] Inflammation of breast tissue, with breast feeding women mostly susceptible.

[48] Area of darker skin around the nipple

[49] Did not attend

[50] X-ray of the breast specially for detecting signs of breast cancer

breast. Biopsies[51] also showed that Ms X had advanced breast cancer which was inoperable, plus secondary cancers of the liver, brain and bone.

The above life changing experience made Ms X to complain to the NHS trust in May 2012 about the care she received. Ms X was particularly keen to know the following:

- How was the diagnosis of mastitis reached? Ms X alleged that Dr A referred to the diagnosis as 'smokers breast'.
- Why was there no further screening/text at the May 2010 appointment when she saw Doctor B?

In its response in July 2012, the NHS trust said Dr A's diagnosis of mastitis was reached through ultrasound scan and clinical examination, pointing out that the scan did not show any signs of malignancy. The trust added that mammography was considered but decided against because patient's breast was sore and swollen, and staff felt the process would have been excessively painful for Ms X.

Regarding appointment with Dr B in May and the fact that no further test was carried out, the NHS trust said Dr B no longer worked for the trust and could not be reached for comments. Notes from that appointment indicated that Dr B considered biopsy but ruled it out on the grounds that it could cause further problems. The trust also argued that the ordering of mammography in this case was a discretionary matter for the clinician, though accepted that it should have been done, with the benefit of hindsight. The trust added that mammography would most likely have been done had the patient attended the appointment scheduled for August 2010.

[51] Tests involving extraction of sample cells or tissues and examining them for infection or disease

Ms X escalated the complaint to the Parliamentary and Health Service Ombudsman (PHSO) which has responsibility for investigating complaints and reaching a decision where a patient or their family remain dissatisfied with the response of the health care provider.

PHSO's findings include:

- Response to Ms X's complaint was inadequate as it failed to recognise failings of the NHS trust and impact of those failings on the patient
- Whilst the clinical care by Dr A was deemed reasonable, failure of Dr B to order test(s) was very much criticised.
- Dr B's new hospital/employer should be advised of the case, to ensure similar errors are not repeated
- When Ms X was discharged from the service in August 2010, the standard, computer generated discharge letter sent to patient and her GP was wholly inadequate. There was no indication that a diagnosis of cancer was a possibility. The diagnosis of mastitis may have given Ms X false sense of relaxation instead of igniting a sense of urgency
- Though the trust has taken appropriate steps to improve its complaint handling, it did not address the unfairness and injustice Ms X suffered not only by the clinical care but also due to how the complaint was managed
- In addition to unequivocal and unreserved apology, PHSO recommended the payment of £70,000 to Ms X as compensation for her pain, suffering, additional medical treatment and distress over a lengthy period caused by service failure.

- Sadly, the position in which Ms X found herself due to the service failures she experienced could not be remedied.

The NHS trust agreed with PHSO's recommendations and complied accordingly.

Case study reflections

Failure to carry out essential or, at the very least, advisable actions in the clinical care given to Ms X sadly left her in a devastating situation that cannot be reversed. Had Dr B thought of the phrase 'better safe than sorry', perhaps she would have ordered diagnostic tests at the May 2010 consultation. Would Ms X not have wanted the choice to endure more pain and distress the diagnostic tests may cause for the price of having better clarity on her condition? Sadly, Dr B made the decision for her, without giving her (Ms X) a say in that decision. Again, a key mantra in health care in the NHS is worth recalling, 'No decision about me without me'.

Did the complaints management provide Ms X some relief or did it add to her frustration? Transparency and the full discharge of the 'Duty of Candour'[52]was sadly lacking.

Did Ms X contribute in any way to the final outcome?

Is the award of £70,000 a fair and proportionate compensation?

---

[52] The duty to be open and transparent, as advocated by Sir Robert Francis KC in his report about the failings at the Mid Staffordshire NHS Foundation trust public inquiry which he chaired

Responding to complaints: Process and time management

The saying 'delay is dangerous' is not always true but does have relevance in nipping a complaint in the bud, responding within agreed timescale, or avoiding the complaint altogether. It is vital that staff on the scene at the time of complaint should show empathy and try to address the complaint or concern there and then, if possible. If unable to do so, the staff should find out the most appropriate staff that can help the patient/complainant and refer appropriately. Telling the patient "Sorry this has nothing to do with my job", "can't help you" or "go make a complaint" does not help and can only add to the frustration of the patient or carer.

Timely response to complaints can also help to reduce the chance of prolonged complaint process. As noted above, timeframe has to be agreed with the patient or whoever is complaining on the patient's behalf at the start of the process, and this should be adhered to.

Should delay become unavoidable, probably due to absence of a key staff involved, the person making the complaint needs to be advised at the earliest opportunity and a revised deadline agreed. Delay in responding to a complaint or lack of communication about likely delay adds to the complainant's feeling of not being taken seriously and can only further aggravate the situation.

See Appendix B for Complaint handling flowchart: Process and time management.

The flowchart helps to manage the entire complaint handling process in order to ensure quality response and minimise the chance of a complaint response breaching the agreed deadline. Note that the complaint handling flowchart as illustrated in appendix B is just one way of managing the process of responding to complaints. This will vary from one healthcare organisation to another, depending on their complaints handling policy. As mentioned earlier in this chapter on the issue of timeframe, some NHS trusts retain the old 25 working days response timeframe whilst some uses 30 working days, and others have multiple response times, based on the complexity of the complaint. The involvement of multiple divisions/services and, in some cases, multiple providers may add a layer of complexity to a complaint. This in turn may make the provider(s) to negotiate for longer response time.

Note that appendix B has four boxes on the right. The second box focuses on examples of issues that may warrant early escalation:

- Legal/Claims
- Safeguarding
- Safety
- Communication/media

As the complaint is being looked at and forwarded to the relevant division for allocation to an investigator, the Complaints team should, at the same time, check if the complaint relates to any issues that may warrant urgent escalation. A complaint letter containing threats of suing the organisation, or perhaps they have already contacted a solicitor, should be immediately brought to the attention of the Legal department for early review. Similarly, if the complaint letter indicates a safeguarding concern relating to a child or vulnerable adult, then such a complaint should be immediately brought to the attention of the Safeguarding team.

The Patient Safety or Clinical Governance team should be alerted to a complaint that is of a serious safety issue, for example a serious harm or fatality. If the complaint letter contains potential reputational damage passed to the media, or threat to involve the media, then the Communications team needs to be alerted at the earliest possible time.

The flowchart in appendix B shows the complaint letter was signed and sent on day 25, leaving five days to spare. The purpose of leaving a few 'spare' days is to make room for likely 'back and forth' that is often unavoidable i.e., the draft letter being sent back for corrections and then re-presented for review and approval. If draft letter was sent back for additional work or corrections on the day it was due to be sent to the complainant, then that complaint deadline would most likely be breached. A breach may further anger the complainant as well as affect the organisation's complaints response rate for that period.

Concerns and Complaints: the dichotomy

To most patients and the public, there is no difference between saying they would like to raise a concern or make a complaint – except in the semantics. Most people use the words 'concerns' and 'complaints' interchangeably. However, there is a significant technical difference between concerns and complaints in the healthcare sector.

- Concerns are usually minor grievances that may be resolved fairly quickly, possibly in just one phone call, minor amendment to a written document, etc. On the other hand, complaints are often serious grievances, and the timeframe for their resolution much longer than that of concerns.
- The resolution of complaints must follow a formal process, starting with a complaint that is usually written, either by the patient/carer or an advocate. On the other hand, concerns can be resolved informally without a written word.
- All concerns have to be resolved locally i.e., by the healthcare organisation concerned. Unlike the management of complaints, there is no second stage such as the referral to the PHSO[53].
- Starting in 2010, complaints data for all NHS hospitals in England is published, allowing for some degree of benchmarking. There is no such data for concerns, partly because of its informal nature.
- Patients, their carers/families and the public should be aware that the process used in addressing the issues they raise – informal concerns or formal complaints – is ultimately theirs to make, though the Complaints/PALS team can guide and suggest the best approach. For example, it is better to address an issue relating to a cancelled appointment through the informal concern/PALS route, especially if the aim is to get the appointment rebooked at the earliest possible time.
- Patients or their families will likely request that their informal concerns are escalated to formal complaints if they get the impression that the issues raised are not being taken seriously.

[53] Parliamentary and Health Service Ombudsman

CASE STUDY 8: Lorry driver surprises Consultant with unarranged visit to the hospital *(North West England)*

A lorry driver was feeling so unwell and so visited his GP[54] who swiftly referred the patient to his local hospital. In turn, the hospital assigned the patient to a Consultant and some tests were ordered. The patient was signed off work but after a couple of weeks, he felt better and wanted to return to work but the Consultant needed to send a note to DVLA[55], certifying him fit to return to work. Weeks flew by and neither the Consultant nor the hospital made any contact with either the patient or his GP[56]. Days turned into weeks, yet no response – despite many reminders sent to the Consultant.

Fed up, bored of sitting at home and unable to earn an income for that period, the lorry driver got frustrated and went straight to the hospital without an appointment. Luckily, he saw the Consultant along one of the hospital's corridors, to the Consultant's shock, suffice to say. The patient later said he wished he had a camera to capture the shock written on the Consultant's face! The patient explained that he was left with no option but to turn up uninvited, due to the long, unexplained delay in getting the requested 'fit to return to work' certification. The Consultant gave the patient the update on his health he wanted to know all along and promised to send a written note to DVLA the following day, and that was done too.

---

[54] General Practioner (primary care doctor)

[55] Driver and Vehicle Licensing Agency is an executive agency of the Department of Transport, UK.

[56] General Practioner (primary care doctor)

Case study reflections

Complete lack of communication, ambiguous communication, insufficient clarity, or delayed communication remains one of the most common issues raised in both formal complaints and informal/PALS concerns. But why is clear, timely, and empathetic communication so challenging for staff in healthcare that the same issues appear stubbornly stuck in the top three themes for complaints and PALS concerns?

Should the driver have turned up at the hospital without an appointment?

What would you advice a loved one to do if they couldn't earn an income, despite feeling well to work and having repeatedly sent reminders?

PALS

The Patient Advice and Liaison Service (PALS) was piloted in 2001 and implemented throughout the NHS by the end of 2002. The main purpose of the service is to provide the private sector's equivalent of customer service whereby patients, their carers and families are provided with any required information and guidance about their local NHS. In addition to signposting and providing other required information and advice, PALS deals with concerns, as described above, ensuring the concerns are logged, satisfactorily addressed, share lessons learned and produce regular reports – usually monthly or quarterly, in addition to annual reports.

It is most reasonable to assert that the PALS team is the 'face' of the healthcare organisation for patients, their carers and families. In most NHS hospitals for example, there is a PALS desk in the main lobby/reception area or other conspicuous and accessible areas on the premises. The desk may sit just one or two staff while the rest of the team may be in a nearby office.

Growing trend: Merging PALS and Complaints into Patient Experience Team

There is a growing trend to merge PALS and Complaints units into Patient Experience Team (PET) or Patient Experience Department (PED). One of the reasons behind this growing trend is the realisation that concerns can easily turn into complaints if not properly managed, so better to keep both units joined-up. The combined team can also help ensure better understanding of complaints, particularly the history of complaints that originated as concerns. There is also the added benefit of lean management and savings as less resources would be required, compared to two separate units.

It is worth stressing that the economic principle of division of labour and specialisation[57] must be applied for better outcomes. So, within the PET or PED[58], there will be staff dedicated to dealing with concerns and some to complaints, with a 'bridging unit' adequately skilled to straddle both ends of the spectrum. This would be a great asset in covering absences, including annual leave and sick leave.

[57] Originally developed by Adam Smith based on his study of a pin making factory.

[58] Patient Experience Team or Patient Experience Department

Instead of different reports, a single report on the 4 Cs will suffice. It is important to identify one or two staff for this task. Good report writing and analytical skills are vital, as well as the ability to effectively use databases and spreadsheets.

So, what does a successful, top performing Patient Experience Department or team look like? What are the key services they should be able to effectively deliver?

- Demonstrate with actions that being part of the organisation does not mean that PED will be partial towards staff. Hence, empathy, openness, fairness and impartiality have to be key guiding principles
- Documenting and explaining the whole process – from acknowledgement to local resolution (or PHSO referral if local resolution could not be achieved).
- Promote the service – not to be a 'lottery discovery' by patients, their families and carers
- Timely acknowledgement and good response rate to complaints
- Involve Executive Board members, ideally the Chief Executive and the Chief Nurse/Director of Nursing in the complaints resolution process. The Chief Executive is ultimately responsible and will often sign (or delegate) the final complaint response letter.
- Robust, easy to use database system
- Use of resolution meetings (face-to-face or virtual) as often as necessary and less dependence on letters alone
- Involvement of an advocacy organisation where the patient is particularly vulnerable (e.g., with Learning Disability) or when requested

- Good communication flow – picking up the phone or quick response to messages is a small but vital step

Patient Experience and the 'Duty of Candour'

There are many patients and their families who doubt the impartiality and fairness of the Patient Experience Department (PED), PALS[59] or Complaints departments of healthcare organisations. One of the main reasons for this doubt is the perception that, being part of the organisation, staff in this department are more likely to protect the interest of their colleagues and image of the organisation at the detriment of the patients' interest. Disclosure of relevant information is often one of the demands of patients when they feel compelled to make a complaint.

Introduced on 1 April 2013 as part of the reforms to the NHS, the 'duty of candour' is designed to instil the culture of transparency and accountability in the fabric of healthcare provision and commissioning. With its roots in the Mid Staffordshire scandal[60], the 'duty of candour' requires patients or their relatives to be advised of any harm or errors in treatment. Same information must also be shared with regulatory and commissioning bodies. This has revolutionised healthcare delivery in the UK, ensuring lessons are learned when things go wrong, rather than sweeping such situations 'under the carpet'[61].

---

[59] Patient Advice and Liaison Service

[60] Failings at the Mid Staffordshire NHS Foundation trust triggered a national inquiry and the Francis Report.

[61] Conceal or ignore

The day-to-day formal application of the 'duty of candour' is more relevant for events that are declared an 'incident', with harm being the most important consideration. However, the overriding ethos of transparency and accountability should be applied to every aspect of care and feedback, including the management of PALS and complaints. On the one hand, it can be used to reassure patients, their carers and families that the Complaints team/PED[62] will get to the bottom of their complaint with transparency and fairness. On the other hand, 'duty of candour' acts as a gentle reminder to any staff or team involved in a complaint or PALS concern to disclose all relevant information.

It is in the interest of every healthcare organisation to ensure that patients, carers and their families have faith and confidence in their PED[63] or Complaints/PALS department, as this would in turn ensure that they are the first port of call for patients. If patients and their carers/families cannot trust PED or Complaints/PALS, they will take their grievances to their local Healthwatch[64], mainstream media, social media platforms, Care Opinion, or their local MP.[65] Should this happen, the healthcare organisation would be forced into a reactive position and would have to be accountable to third parties, in addition, with potentially damaging consequences.

---

[62] Patient Experience Department

[63] ditto

[64] Healthwatch came into being in England from 1 April 2013, replacing LINks (Local Involvement Networks). They were set up by statutory instrument to act as a conduit between patients/service users and providers/commissioners of health and social care services.

[65] Member of Parliament in the House of Commons, UK

Top Complaints: Common themes in complaints and concerns

The themes that feature prominently and frequently in NHS complaints and concerns data include communication, attitude/behaviour, clinical care, cancelled or delayed appointments and discharge arrangements.

Concerns/complaints /compliments received trust wide in Quarter 3 (October – December) – Data from an NHS trust in South East England

- Concerns/queries raised and dealt with informally = 901
- Complaints (managed formally) = 164
- Compliments received = 3,322
- Compliments to complaints ratio = 20:1
- No. of new referrals to PHSO = 22
- % of formal complaints in relation to total spells of care (in-patients and outpatients) = 0.09% (i.e., 1 formal complaint per 1114 recorded spells of care)

TABLE OF FORMAL & INFORMAL COMPLAINTS INVOLVING DOCTORS/CONSULTANTS IN A THREE-MONTH PERIOD (QUARTER 3: OCTOBER – DECEMBER)

Data from an NHS Foundation trust in South East England

THEMES	FREQUENCY
Problems with treatment/care	29
Problems with communication	18

Problems with diagnosis	18
Problems with attitude/behaviour	13
Delays	11
Concerns about surgical management	10
Problems with medication	9
Problems with discharge arrangements	8
Concerns about clinical management	3
Infection control and prevention	1
Enquiry clarification or admin query	1
Cancellations	1
Privacy and dignity issues	1

Total no. of formal complaints = 123

Total no. of concerns (informal) = 125

CASE STUDY 9: "The foetus is shrinking" … but all that followed was silence *(London)*

With less than two months to the expected delivery date, a woman expecting her first child was advised at a London hospital that measurements just taken showed her unborn baby was "shrinking"! Despite the capacity of this brief statement to devastate any expectant mother, there was no communication as to why or what will be done. There was no sign of the Consultant that was supposed to explain the situation and likely next steps. This naturally worried the patient a lot, so she discussed the situation with her sister who happened to be a GP[66]. The sister researched the possible causes of the reported "shrinking" and found that there was a chance the said "shrinking" could be due to nothing more than incorrect measurement. The sister was able to calm down the new mother-to-be, thereby preventing any potential complication that could arise due to high stress level and panicking.

The expectant mother was eventually told, after three days that there was nothing to worry about – it was only a measurement error! The expectant mother was, first and foremost, very relieved but also angry that she was giving such a news which could have ended differently without any sign of urgency to explain possible causes, effects and what that could mean for the unborn baby. If not for her sister who helped prevent her worries and anxiety from 'going through the roof', perhaps the clinicians would have had a real complication to worry about.

Due to the overall good care and support she received, the patient did not make a formal complaint but raised the issue as an informal concern.

Case study reflections

A lot can go wrong with our health, so being in relatively good health is great news. Same is true of the unborn child. What emotions do we then have to deal with when advised of the possibility of something going wrong with our health, or that of a foetus or unborn child? Not only should staff in any care setting be cognisant of how such news is delivered, but more importantly must not create a

[66] General Practioner, primary care doctor

communication vacuum. Follow-up information on next steps and support should help reassure patients and their carers/families.

Was it professional and helpful for a suspected worrisome development to be presented as it was done in this case, with the tone of finality and certainty?

What possible scenarios could have played out if the expectant mother didn't get the calming 'pat on the shoulder' and support from her sister?

Tips on how to reduce complaints and increase compliments

How lovely would the world of healthcare completely devoid of complaints be? Ask a Ward Manager in any hospital and he/she would breathe the loudest sigh of relief imaginable. Whilst zero complaint is mere wishful thinking, practical steps can be taken to bring complaints to the barest minimum while increasing the level of compliments. The answer does not rest on manipulative practices, such as complicating the complaints process in order to frustrate patients or carers that may wish to complain or hiding away the complaints team and their contact details. Such manipulation can only worsen the situation.

Practical steps that can help in achieving high compliments-complaints ratio includes the following:

Learning from previous complaints/concerns is vital. It is sad to note that themes of most common complaints tend to remain largely unchanged in many healthcare organisations. This is partly due to the fact that the process of learning from that complaint or theme of complaints has either not been looked into or done as a short-term fix. To effectively learn from complaints so as to significantly reduce reoccurrence, the following steps must be actioned:

- Investigate and understand what went wrong
- Develop and implement an action plan to bring about needed improvements.
- How can this problem be prevented from reoccurring? This would be more challenging, long-term fix if it relates to staff attitude or communication, and much easier to fix if the complaint was about a faulty door lock or equipment, for example. So be realistic about expectations and timeframe.
- Create a 'Change Register' for recording the problem and solution linked to a complaint or series of complaints
- Share the problem and solution throughout the organisation – website/intranet, ward and departmental meetings and briefings, inductions, training, etc.
- Thank the patient or carer that complained and inform them of the steps taken, with reassurance that you're doing everything possible to prevent its reoccurrence
- Embed the solution through regular reminders and monitoring – especially if behavioural or attitudinal problem.

Apology

A manager in the NHS who was previously working in the insurance sector once spoke about his difficulty in transitioning from not apologising and admitting fault to that of apologising to patients when they had cause to complain or raise a concern.

There is a common assumption that apologising to a patient, their family or carer is the same thing as accepting fault and responsibility for failure. This assumption is simply wrong.

Experience in complaints processing and management shows that many patients and their families simply want the healthcare organisation to know and appreciate what they have been through, physically or emotionally, and seeking assurance that it won't happen again. In vast majority of cases, complaint responses that apologises, at least for the fact that the patient or relative felt the need to complain in the first instance, and reassures them with concrete examples that the issues raised are being taken seriously are more likely to achieve resolution than responses that are very defensive and unapologetic.

Whilst it is important to stress that the full facts of a complaint can only become known after a thorough investigation, staff should be made aware that it is ok for them to say sorry to patients/carers who felt let down.

The Ombudsman (PHSO) found that culture in the NHS made it difficult for patients who suffered harm to get the apology they deserve.[67]

The other point is that they should not say 'this will never happen again' in all cases, as cast-iron guarantee cannot be given in cases involving staff attitude, for example. Instead, staff should say something to the effect that all necessary steps are being taken or will be taken to prevent reoccurrence.

---

[67] The findings of a review conducted by the Parliamentary and Health Service Ombudsman (PHSO) on the 'Quality of NHS complaints investigations'

It is not uncommon to find ward clerks, nurses, doctors and other patient-facing staff subjected to abuse. Though many NHS hospitals have 'zero tolerance' policy designed to protect their staff from abuse from patients or visitors, most times staff don't report abusive behaviour, especially from patients. In a few cases, unruly or abusive patients realise their mistakes and apologise.

CASE STUDY 10: "People sometimes misbehave when in pain" *(London)*

This was the confession and 'let's make up' comment of an in-patient at a London NHS hospital. The patient had 'earned' a bad reputation among staff the previous day and the nursing staff pre-warned their colleagues that are likely to work in the bay where this patient was. The patient lived up to his not-too-good reputation when one HCA[68] went to attend to him. Realising he had been unfair to the HCA and a few other nursing staff on the ward, the patient started being very friendly with greetings like 'hello my friend', 'how are you nurse?'. As the HCA concerned was making her way home after three consecutive days of 12-hour shifts, the patient called out 'Bye nurse...thank you nurse and then made the remark "people sometimes misbehave when in pain" and went on to apologise. The HCA concerned was happy she had remained professional and exercised patience with this patient.

[68] Health Care Assistant

Case study reflections

Virtually all NHS hospitals have a 'zero tolerance' for staff abuse or assault. Patient can be issued with verbal and later written warnings. The ultimate penalty, in exceptional circumstances, could see the patient barred from attending the hospital, except in an emergency. That said, staff often overlook cases of patients' bad behaviour as they strive to preserve good professional relationship with their patients. But where do you draw the line? When do you say, 'enough is enough'? Thankfully, some patients realise their excesses and apologise before things get out of hand, as in the case above.

Smile

The calming impact of a smile in a stressful situation such as hospital clinic consultation or procedure is known by many but practised by relatively few staff in the healthcare sector. It is not uncommon for staff themselves to be stressed by long hours of work and the sheer physical and emotional stress that goes with the job, hence smiling does not often come naturally to healthcare staff. This is where patient experience comes in – stressing and reminding staff of the need to smile, alongside others measures that can contribute to a patient's positive experience.

Please see chapter 5 for case study 11: Go the Extra Smile!

Sharing best practice and feedback

One of the proven ways for improving quality of healthcare services is through the sharing of best practice and feedback, with the latter including compliments, complaints/concerns, their resolution and lessons learnt.

What tends to happen in most healthcare organisations, especially the large ones, is that compliments, comments, concerns and complaints and lessons learnt from them are shared with the Board of Directors and senior management but not shared with the patient-facing staff that arguably needs to know the most.

Just as the brightest light hidden and covered up is of little use, so also is the futility of not sharing widely the best practice and lessons learnt from the 4 Cs[69].

Rewards and reprimand (Operant conditioning)

The consequences of behaviour determine the probability that the behaviour will occur again[70]

B F Skinner
(1904 – 1990)
American Psychologist

Behavioural psychology has enriched our understanding of human behaviour, and this understanding has impacted upon every facet of our lives, from consumerism to motivation in the workplace. Skinner's operant conditioning uses reinforcement and punishment to create associations between behaviour and their consequences. Applied to patient experience, staff who make an already stressful

[69] Complaints, concerns, comments and compliments.

[70] Skinner based his work on operant conditioning on Thorndike's Law of Effect (1898) www.simplypsycology.org (Accessed 28 June 2023)

situation even more stressful for patients and their families should be reprimanded or punished, depending on the severity of their actions, if their employers would like the chance of repeating such a behaviour to be less likely in future.

Conversely, employers can increase the chances of a behaviour that earn compliments from patients and their families/carers being repeated if such behaviour was rewarded. The reward can range from a simple verbal acknowledgement to a letter from the trust Chair or Chief Executive, the presentation of a divisional special award certificate, gift or plaque.

Patient experience training, especially for front line staff

Training in patient experience should be mandatory for all staff in health organisations, both clinical and administrative. A receptionist or ward clerk who is disrespectful to patients or their families/carers can, to some extent, undo the good works of the best surgeons or nurses.

Using staff inductions, ward/team briefings and regular training sessions to remind and update staff on patient experience would go a long way in keeping fresh in their memory, and therefore very likely in their behaviour, the importance of dignity, respect and empathy for patients, their carers, and families.

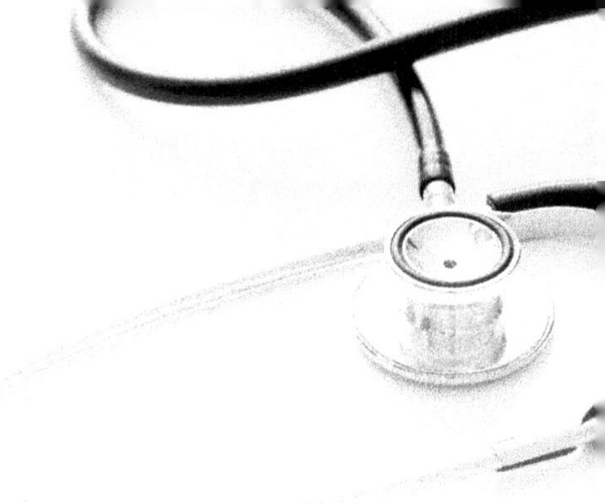

CHAPTER FOUR

Using data to improve services: Now that you know, what are you going to do about it?

This chapter reinforces the message that the gathering of patient experience data is not an end in itself but part of a process for achieving positive patient experience. Data analysis, interpretation, and reporting are relevant here. Does the data show trends and themes? Should the survey report be selectively circulated among staff, or should it be accessible to all staff? Patients' cooperation made the research possible, so should the report be openly available to patients and the public too? What steps should be taken to ensure that poor scores are turned around as soon as practically possible? This is the essence of evidence-based health care in the field of patient experience.

Getting patient feedback regularly is fast becoming the norm in healthcare delivery and commissioning in the UK. What is still not the norm is using the gathered information to improve services. But why is that? Surely, after expending money, time, and human resources in gathering information about the experiences of patients from different sources, as identified in chapters 2 and 3, the effort must count for something tangible.

Regrettably, instances of unused feedback data archived on computer hard drives and store cupboards still abound. Failure to understand the positive outcomes the use of patient feedback can deliver often result in low priority for this task. In some cases, the data may have been collected for the wrong reasons - 'tick box' exercise, to do as others are doing and meet guidelines and legal requirements. Organisations that gather data on patient experience for such frivolous reasons are not likely to take the process to its logical conclusion i.e., using analysed data to improve services.

What should be done with the gathered data on patient experience? The end point has to be service improvement and increased patient satisfaction. So, what are the key stages between the gathering of data and this desired result?

The key stages should include the following:

- Collation of data – quantitative and qualitative
- Data analysis, identifying trends and themes
- Developing action plans
- Assigning ownership for specific aspects while 'all hands remain on deck'

- Board endorsement
- Disseminating key messages to all staff, with regular reminders
- Embed changes

Collation of data

The first stage after collecting primary[71] data is to collate the data. This simply means pulling the data together and organising it in a way that makes it easier to use e.g., arranging them according to the corresponding questions.

Good data analysis that can identify trends and themes and have a great potential in transforming services must first be well collated, otherwise the data would be mixed up and would be useful only to those keen on comparing apples and oranges![72]

After data collation, then the data can be analysed.

Data analysis and identifying trends and themes - quantitative and qualitative

Analysis is usually done quantitatively or qualitatively, depending on the nature of the data. Where the type of data lends itself more to quantitative (numerical) analysis, it is recommended that an element of qualitative analysis is also added to bring deeper meaning to the figures.

[71] Data obtained from field research, in this case from patients and carers – as against secondary data obtained from books, internet or other sources.

[72] A common idiom referring to invalid comparisons. Comparing items that are not suitable for comparison.

This is why it is recommended, in chapter 2, that 'open ended' questions are introduced in questionnaires to enable respondents to be able to comment in their own words about their experiences rather than just box ticking throughout. While the data from box ticking is best analysed quantitatively, insights from comments is best analysed qualitatively.

For organisations that opt to collect data using digital technologies, the data can be collated and analysed much more quickly and possibly in real time. The speed of data collation and analysis is one of the key selling points for the use of IT[73] in this process. Web-based systems are now commonplace, with surveys completed on handheld or kiosk electronic devices and enabling speedy data analysis and reporting in real time.

What is the distribution pattern of the data? In other words, what are the most and least popular responses and what message is emerging from those responses? For example, if 80% of respondents identify the same cause of concern, say staff attitude, then that becomes a key theme that must be noted. A trend will emerge when we study the responses on the theme of staff attitude more closely. Are there certain distinguishing characteristics among staff whose attitude raise concern? Are they mostly staff on a particular ward? Are they senior or relatively junior staff? Do they work day or night shift? Teasing out common denominators among staff whose attitude are raising concern will give us a much deeper understanding of the subject, and therefore a better chance of developing action plans with a high chance of effectively addressing staff attitude concerns.

[73] Information Technology

Any worth for statistically insignificant data?

If 2 out of 2000 (0.1%) respondents identify a concern, that concern may not be statistically significant and so may have a very low priority, or none, in terms of areas to focus on. But that's only if the analyst is merely skimming the surface. It is not impossible for only 2 out of 2000 people to identify a very key issue worthy of attention. This could be because of the specialist knowledge of the 2 people or perhaps they have unique experiences that could help prevent a serious problem in future, if taken seriously. For example, if the respondents turn out to be 2 out of only 6 disabled or minority ethnic respondents in the sample, then suddenly the 0.1% becomes 33.3% for that particular demographic, and therefore very significant statistically.

Developing action plans

Once the issues that are of concern to most patients and their families have been identified, the next stage is to plan how to tackle those issues and improve services. To develop action plans, the best possible action has to be agreed for each area of concern or theme. The chance of getting this right will be enhanced if a steering group is set up for this. By bringing together key people with the relevant roles, skills and experience for the issues being addressed, the more robust the action plan is likely to be, especially if patients/service users and their carers are represented. Though two heads are not necessarily better than one, but one could reasonably argue that two good heads are often better than one good head!

In addition, a realistic time frame needs to be agreed. Agreeing a deadline by which certain plans should be actioned helps to focus minds. Though certain actions may have their deadline as 'ongoing', experience shows that some managers state "ongoing" as deadlines where a specific date could be determined, so as to avoid having overdue actions.

Assigning ownership while all hands remain on deck

Equally important in developing action plans is the need to identify the person to lead on each strand of the action plan. This should never be interpreted to mean that it is solely the responsibility of the named individual; team work remains vital. The lead however has the additional task of pulling all the 'strings' together, to deliver the set objective within the agreed timescale.

Board endorsement

Hierarchy is a vivid feature of most organisations, though some claim to be non-hierarchical. In the healthcare sector, and more particularly in the NHS, hierarchy does not just exist, it is woven into the fabric of most organisations and very much respected. At the very top of the hierarchical structure is the board, comprising of both the executive management, the non-executive directors and headed by the Chair.

To demonstrate a strong resolve in turning patient experience data into improved services and patient satisfaction level, the board needs to back the action plan. This could be through one of its committees or the involvement of an executive director. This approach helps to put the 'seal of approval' on the work and secure commitment from staff to deliver their part of the action plan efficiently and in a timely fashion.

It is not uncommon to see key projects fall apart simply due to the lack of visible support and sponsorship of a director or senior executive. Due to the overwhelming work pressure in hospitals and other health care organisations, the priority and commitment staff give to projects is directly proportional to the level of seniority of the person leading or supporting it. So, where the Chair, Chief Executive, or a Director has thrown the weight of the board behind an action plan or project, staff commitment can be safely guaranteed.

Disseminating key messages to all staff, with regular reminders

It is not enough to communicate the key messages from an action plan with the board and top executives. Engaging with the entirety of the work force, especially patient-facing staff should be non-negotiable.

There are usually 'quick wins' where a sign needs to be put up or an equipment repaired or purchased. However, similar quick fix does not apply where culture and staff attitude need to change. As noted above, action plans relating to a change in attitude is difficult to fix. The complexity of human behaviour means health organisations must be ready to be persistently determined to achieve desired changes.

Having a big launch and a publicity 'burst' is great but that must be complemented with a long-term plan involving effective staff engagement, regular reminders, and monitoring. Having one major event to publicise the problem and actions required but with no follow up is a common error in addressing attitudinal problems in organisations.

Action plans and the recommended actions should be made available to patients and the public, except there is a valid reason why this should be kept an internal document. The support of patients and the public made data collection possible, so demonstrating that you've listened and prepared to make the necessary changes is important for a number of key reasons:

Firstly, showing you have listened and willing to make changes where necessary will serve as a motivating factor for patients, carers, and the public to want to engage with the healthcare organisation and provide feedback in future.

Secondly, it serves as 'checks and balances', as staff are aware that patients and the public know what they should be doing and what they shouldn't. Imagine a world where pupils don't know the limitations of teachers and the public don't know the limitations of Police Officers. Giving wide, public access to what is expected of staff and what is not permissible means that staff are more likely to be adherent.

Embed changes

This is the step that separates the winners from the 'also-rans'[74]. To ensure the work that started with surveys and other forms of data

[74] Losers

collection is taken to its logical conclusion, changes implemented must be embedded.

One way of embedding changes is regular monitoring. To avoid predictable inspection routine, a staggered approach is recommended. In other words, staff cannot be at their best behaviour and ensure everything is where they should be, just to get a 'thumbs up' for the inspection. Regular but not always predictable monitoring regime is the winning way. Use of unannounced visits and inspections should complement regular, known inspections.

Who should be involved in the monitoring and inspections? Again, the wider the mix, the better. It is most helpful to have a combination of clinicians, managers/administrators as well as patients and carers.

Monitoring and inspections are great but will not suffice. Operant conditioning, as discussed in Chapter 3, should be applied to embed good practice. Good practice and constant adherence should be rewarded – from verbal commendation to special awards. Conversely, utter disregard for guidelines, bye laws and code of conduct should be met with disapproval – from verbal warnings to disciplinary measures.

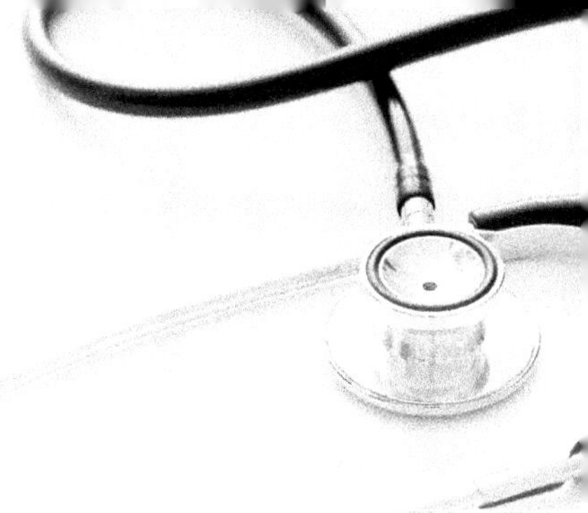

CHAPTER FIVE

The synergy effect: Patient experience, patient/ public engagement, and communications

This chapter explores the complementary nature of communications (particularly health communications), patient experience, patient/public engagement, involvement, co-production, and staff engagement. We also explore the strength and challenges of patient/public engagement and involvement as a tool for enhancing patient experience.

Who knows best? Doctors, nurses and other healthcare professionals and administrators on the one hand or patients, their families, carers, and the public on the other? Who knows where the shoe hurts the most? Could that be the person wearing the shoe or the cobbler that makes or repairs the shoe? Could there be any sense in recognising that there is a different but equally relevant 'expertise' in both camps?

Most of the greatest challenges confronting societies and the human race have been overcome by teams, communities, or nations coming together to combat a common threat – from World Wars to terrorism, and from climate change to pandemics. Similarly, in healthcare, better outcomes can be achieved when Patient Experience is well aligned with other teams such as Communications (Public Relations/Marketing Communications), Patient/Public Engagement and Involvement, Clinical Governance, Safeguarding, and Claims/ Legal. If we strip out the labels, there are many commonalities between health communications, patient experience, and patient/public engagement and involvement than are immediately recognisable. It is therefore imperative that these teams should not work in silos if optimum output is to be achieved.

The synergy

The practice of public relations (PR) and the wider marketing communications have been established as professional disciplines many decades before the relatively new emergence of patient experience on the professional landscape. That said, communications, particularly health communications and patient experience are not mutually exclusive. The similarities become more apparent when you consider patient/public engagement and involvement as often twinned with patient experience. Among the key functions of communications is stakeholder relations which is broadly categorised into internal and external stakeholders. In health communications, patients are one major stakeholder, alongside the Non-Executive Directors (NEDs), the local Clinical Commissioning Group (CCG) who commissions and pays for the services, the Care

Quality Commission (CQC) who regulates and inspects health services, the media, and others.

One of the remits of the Patient Experience team is to organise the sharing of patient stories at board meetings, thereby bringing alive the high-level data on patient experience that are regularly sent to the board. Through the sharing of patient stories, members of the board (executive and non-executive members) get to hear from 'the horse's mouth', with all the emotions and reality-check the stories bring. PR and health communication professionals would be forgiven for thinking this remit was cut out of their job descriptions.

Just as PR professionals would find opinion shapers, or influencers, to use a social media parlance, to help influence a stakeholder and better align their positions, similarly patient experience professionals use patient representatives, patient forums, and patient experience champions (among staff) to shape patients' opinions. Patient and public involvement provides a rich source of intelligence on the views of patients, their carers and families, and thereby give health organisations the advance notice to respond by addressing the concerns and communicating the outcomes.

Finding out patients' views, compliments, concerns, and complaints is a very vital function of patient experience (as shown in chapter 3). By extension, use of survey is a standard tool in patient/public engagement and involvement, just as it is in communications, and stakeholder relations in particular. It is common sense that you can only address the issues you are aware of. The data generated through surveys, comments, compliments, concerns, and complaints helps in service improvements, design of new services, and the redesign of existing services.

CASE STUDY 11:
Go the extra smile! *(South West England)*

The Patient Experience team at a hospital was receiving concerns about staff looking as if they would rather be anywhere else. Patients and their families were stressing the impact the look on the faces of staff was having on them, considering most of them were already very anxious and in some cases scared of the news they might receive from diagnostic tests done or worrying as they think of a procedure they are about to undergo. What started as isolated concerns later grew to many concerns regularly reported by patients, their families, and carers. It became obvious to the Patient Experience team that something needed to be done.

The solution was the joined-up plan between the Patient Experience team and the NHS trust's Communications team. A campaign was developed with the theme 'Go the Extra Smile' and was launched across the hospital sites, using posters, trust intranet and internet, as well as other digital platforms such as computer desktops. Within a few weeks of the campaign, gradual decline in the number of concerns raised was noticed. This got even better as time went on.

The trust was able to advise patients and their loved ones raising the concerns about what was being done to address the issue, and the regular improvement being reported. This was of course reassuring for patients and families, and the issue that was once a concern started to become a central theme for compliments – comforting and assuring smile!

Case study reflections

Ever felt welcome and reassured by a radiant smile? Not only does smile help to calm nerves and reassure, it can be infectious too! 'Avoid catching an infection' is a good advice but smile is an exception to that rule. It is fair to admit that smile does not come naturally to the face of a tired and exhausted nurse, doctor, ward clerk, or any other staff in a care setting – that takes a lot of effort and professionalism. The reward of smiling must be the focus for staff. If it calms the nerves of already anxious patients and their loved ones, it must be worth the effort.

How to engage and involve patients and local communities

Engaging and involving patients, their carers and families is not only good practice for providers and commissioners of health care services in the UK; it is also obligatory and a legal duty.

There is no one way of engaging and involving patients and public. Instead, there are many options available, and each organisation can decide how they choose to go about it.

What is important is that patients, their carers/families, and local communities have a platform to express their views of what is working well or what they are happy with, as well as challenges or things that needs to change. Importantly, engagement and involvement must be a two-way communication: You said, we did; or could not do because of 'factors A and B'.

ENGAGEMENT CONTINUUM: FROM MAKING CONTACT TO CO-PRODUCTION

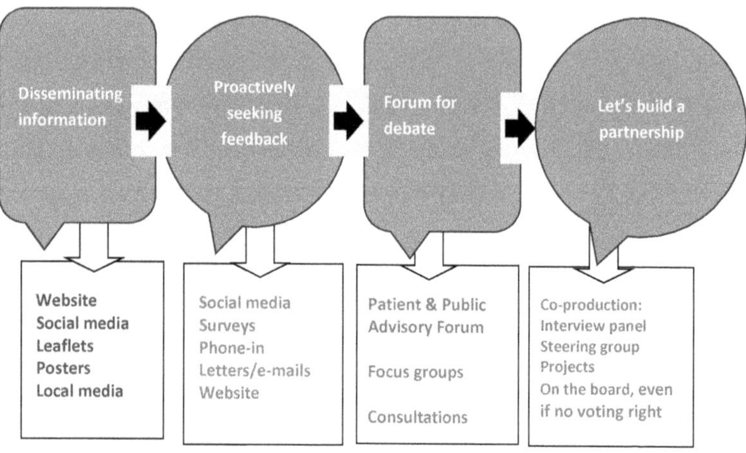

The above diagram shows the engagement-partnership/co-production continuum, from the giving of information to full participation and the stages in between. Each stage has its own key functions and limitations until the participation stage is reached.

The continuum also shows the crossover point, where engagement translates to involvement. It should be noted that involvement has to be strategy-driven, purposeful and selective, hence an organisation may move relationship from engagement to involvement for certain purposes, at certain times and for specific stakeholders whilst maintaining engagement with other stakeholders. In relationships of health care organisations with patients and public, a key distinguishing feature of involvement is when partnership is developed. This could be by way of service users getting involved in the recruitment of contractors or staff, or being involved on a co-design project, e.g., working with the organisation to review a service pathway and make necessary changes for improved services.

The engagement-involvement dichotomy is not exclusive to health care. The same concept applies to many other professions and sectors. Ferlazzo (2011)[75] used the dichotomy to explain teachers' relationships with the parents of their students, stressing that "enlisting parents as partners in the educational process" often yield better dividends for the students' progress in school.

Let us examine each stage in turn.

Giving information: one-directional communication

This is the most basic stage of engagement, where information about a project, a business plan or about an organisation is giving out. This could be done using multiple ways, including the use of flyers, websites, social media, and word of mouth.

Depending on the way the giving out of information is done, it is possible to give information without enabling the giving of feedback on the information received. In such a case, the information flow is one-directional and therefore the sender does not know whether the information given was understood, and the comments the receiver would like to make.

Receiving feedback: two-directional communication

In this case, the sender of the information has consciously built-in a way through which the information receiver can give feedback.

[75] Larry Ferlazzo's article titled 'Involvement or Engagement?' (2011)

Most websites, for example, have the 'Contact us' page that allows the site visitor/information receiver to respond. The response could of course be positive/complimentary or negative. Feedback could also be neutral, such as making comments/suggesting ideas. Most other media channels support the giving of feedbacks such as 'send back' forms that you can tear of a newspaper/magazine advert or advertorial, audience phone in on radio/TV shows, and 'likes' and 'share' on social media platforms such as Twitter and Facebook.

Forums for debate

This is a level up, compared to the receiving of feedback. Creating a platform, either face-to-face or online, for open discussions and critique of a plan, a draft strategy or planned service changes. Here, the giving of information, receiving of feedback and having discussion to assess the pros and cons of any new idea or proposed patient pathway changes all happen in a 'one stop' fashion. Negative feedback should not necessarily mean abandoning planned changes or ideas but should be seen as an opportunity to go back to the 'drawing board' and modify the plan accordingly. Changes should be done only after making further enquiries and reassured that the opinions expressed are indeed valid and widespread. Making a complete u-turn and abandoning a proposed change should also not be ruled out if further research and impact analysis support such a position.

Participation/partnership

This is arguably the phase where patient and public engagement transforms into co-production, the ultimate in patient/public engagement. In other words, this phase turns patients and their carers into partners who work with the organisation to enhance patient experience. Examples may include working with staff to conduct ward rounds/inspections, sitting on interview panels, or sitting on a steering group for a specific project. Some NHS organisations have a patient/carer representative sit on their board where they contribute to discussions, though without a voting right.

CASE STUDY 12: Lack of communication scuppers patient's last wish[76] *(Wales)*

Enjoy the sight of our newly beautified garden before you die. This was the wish of the husband of a patient dying of cancer who was about to be transported by an ambulance from a hospice to her home, to die in the comfort of her home and with her loved ones by her bedside.

Mr Y (husband) was given the date and time when his wife would be brought home, in line with her wishes. The ambulance arrival time at their home was confirmed as 4.30pm on a summer evening.

Knowing that the one thing his wife would really love was a well-presented garden, Mr Y embarked on the beautification of their front garden, so that he could pleasantly surprise his wife with the warm welcome and love that the beautiful garden would convey. He knew that this was guaranteed to cheer her up and brighten her face.

[76] Source: 1000 Lives of Fywydau, Wales, UK

So, the countdown to that fateful day was over, and the countdown to the time of 4.30pm began...tick...tick...tick.

The arrival time of 4.30pm was here but there was no arrival of Mrs Y. A little delay maybe...then it was 5.00pm...tick...tick... 6.00pm... still his wife did not arrive. With no one calling Mr Y to explain the cause of the delay, he embarked on frantic attempts to contact the hospice and the Ambulance trust to find out what was going on but no answers, only appeals for patience....and more patience as time ticks on. Then it was 7.00pm .... 8.00pm ....9.00pm ...and still no sign of an ambulance to bring home his dying wife. Then of course day was beginning to give way to night, and soon the whole grand surprise to make his wife see the beautiful front garden as they wheel her into their home was beginning to fade. Another round of calls by Mr Y to get update were futile. Then it was 10.00pm...11.00pm...and still no sign of an ambulance or any vehicle parking in front of the house.

The ambulance finally pulled up in front of the house at almost 1.00am. It was very dark as the ambulance crew wheeled Mrs Y into her home, with her horrified and extremely disappointed husband there to welcome his wife home...but of course it was way too dark for his dying wife to see the beautiful front garden he worked so hard on, as a special parting gift to his dying wife. She died six days later and never saw the garden because her health had deteriorated so much.

Mr Y put in a complaint about this incident, stressing that he would have been happy to make arrangements for a private ambulance had he been informed there was or likely to be a problem in transporting his wife home at the time given or thereabout. He was disappointed about the very long delay as he was about the total lack of communication.

Reflection on case study

This case shows the importance of communication and engagement with patients and their carers/families. Not only did the service of transporting patient home had much to be desired due to long delay but there was complete lack of communication. As the husband stated, he would have been happy to privately arrange transport to bring his wife home, if only someone bothered to communicate and engage with him on the problem the Ambulance Service was having at the time.

The complaints and PALS[77] data of many NHS trusts support the notion that the lack of communication is often in the top three themes. Improving communication should therefore be a priority for the enhancement of patient experience.

Examples of engagement/involvement platforms

Patient forums

Forums are a popular way of engaging with patients/service users and their carers. A forum is essentially a group of patients and carers who meet regularly, usually monthly (could be every other month or quarterly) to discuss issues relating to health care services they

[77] Patient Advice and Liaison Service

receive, staffing issues, or anything that may directly or indirectly affect patients, their carers/families and visitors. Non-clinical issues that may attract the attention of forums may include parking, food, and patient confidentiality.

Forums may be organised for the whole organisation, such as an NHS trust, a division or directorate such as Medicine and Urgent Care, or a specific service or speciality such as ENT (Ear, Nose, and Throat).

Forum meetings and events will normally be attended by some staff members who are expected to ensure that suggestions and recommendations are considered for implementation. There should also be feedback to the forum on actions taken, recommendations that could not be taken forward, and why.

Appointing patient representatives to sit on committees or steering groups

Deliberating and planning with staff and patients/carers sitting side-by-side is a powerful mechanism for ensuring the views and concerns of patients and carers are well considered at the planning stage, thereby avoiding potential challenges from patient groups and advocacy organisations at a much later stage when changes to the plan may be more difficult and expensive. In appointing patient representatives to join a steering group or task and finish group, it is worth considering lived experience, special interests, or circumstances of the patient representative, to ensure they can add value to the group.

On average, most groups tend to be a minimum of five members and not likely to be more than 20, if that many. In the author's work experience, average membership size of steering groups ranges from 8 – 15. So, some level of proportionality is worth considering in terms of the number of patient representatives to bring on board. Whilst one patient representative should suffice for a group of five, for example, the same number would be insufficient for a group of 15 – for the latter group, the author suggests a minimum of three patient/carer representatives.

Obtaining patient feedback from the local Healthwatch

This is another way of having patient input into the work of an NHS trust or any other health and care organisation. Healthwatch is a statutory body that serves as a conduit between patients/public on one hand and government-funded health and care providers/ commissioners on the other. In addition to Healthwatch England, there are local Healthwatch which are mostly coterminous with local councils. They work to ensure the voice of patients, residents of care homes, and their carers/families are heard and taken seriously.

Working with Voluntary Community and Social Enterprise (VCSE) sector

Local voluntary and social enterprise organisations have great deal of expertise in the areas they focus on and are a great resource to complement work of the NHS and government departments responsible for social care services, including local councils. For example, a major review of services for older people may be missing a critical link if the local Age UK or any other established charity caring for older people is not engaged with. From focused disease conditions to wellness and horticulture, there are dedicated VCSE organisations worth partnering with.

Events

Events is a fantastic opportunity to bring together staff, patients, forum members/patient representatives, local Healthwatch, as well as local VCSE organisations. The health and care provider organisation can use the event to get instant feedback from attendees on new services, plans to redesign services, planned closures, major new facilities or equipment, etc. The sitting arrangement could be such that each table would have a mixture of patients, patient representatives, staff and VCSE organisations. Discussions and key points from each table can then be presented and all points captured for review and consideration.

Events can also provide immediate opportunities for networking, recruitment of volunteers and forum members, having stalls for raising awareness of services, presentations for providing updates about developments and generally raising profile of the health and care organisation.

Social media platforms

Using social media platforms such as Facebook, Twitter, TikTok, YouTube, Instagram and What'sApp can be effective ways of engaging with patients, their carers, and families, particularly the younger people who source most of their information from social media and websites.

Benefits of patient/public engagement and involvement

Engaging patients and public is critical in the management of any health care organisation or practice. It should therefore be planned, strategic and well thought through and not done simply because an organisation wants to create a façade or just wants to be seen as conforming to best practice without having a meaningful engagement strategy.

There are benefits that makes patient/public engagement and involvement very beneficial and worth the investment of human resources, time, and money. Below are some of benefits:

Fulfilling statutory obligations

In the UK, engaging patients and the public is a statutory obligation. Patients have a right to be heard.

Major developments in patient and public involvement in England includes:

- The establishment of Community Health Councils (CHCs,1974)
- Health and Social Care Act 2001
- Creation of the Commission for Patient and Public Involvement in Health (CPPIH, 2003)

- Patient and Public Involvement Forums (2003)
- Local Involvement Networks (2008)
- NHS Constitution (first published in 2009)
- The Health and Social Act 2012
- Healthwatch England (2013)
- Local Healthwatch (2013)

Promoting openness and accountability

Developing structures and processes for promoting involvement and the ultimate of co-production have at its very heart the art of outcome-oriented dialogue and idea sharing from a level-playing, non-hierarchical platform where experts by experience (i.e., people with lived experience of physical or mental health conditions), and their carers sit side-by-side with service managers and clinicians.

Discussions may revolve around questions such as: What you wish to do? Why do you want to do it? What impact would it have on different groups of patients? What resources are needed? What gaps exist between resources required and resources currently available? How would it be implemented? How would it be assessed and monitored? Would it be done virtually or in person? If in person, where would it be based? These are some of the many questions that would be brainstormed over. Therefore, transparency and accountability cannot be compromised.

Good source of intelligence that can help to defuse tensions and avoid complaints

Patient and public involvement is a rich source of intelligence through which a health or social care organisation can have their ears to the ground and feel the pulse of their communities. Through patient and carer forums of various descriptions, health and social care organisations have a better chance of getting information they would otherwise not get, and therefore have the advantage of reacting quickly to defuse tension and resolve brewing problems before they become crystallised or lead to formal complaints.

Improving the planning of and access to services

Involving patients and carers in service planning, redesign and improvement efforts fosters the sharing of experiences, including initiatives that worked well and those that patients and service users find challenging. The feedback obtained from involvement will go a long way in informing service providers on segments of the patient population that are struggling to access services. This may be due to language barriers and inadequacy of the translation and interpretation services, gender reassignment, racial barriers, or any of the other protected characteristics.

Creating positive patient experience

The very fact that a service provider engages with patients, residents, and carers improve trust and the feeling of being valued and respected. The higher the level of engagement, the easier and quicker concerns are likely to be resolved, and the stronger the feeling of being valued and respected. This will often enhance a positive patient experience.

Enabling patients and public to have a say about health planning, design and provision: "No decision about me without me"[78]

In the UK, there is a legal obligation on the part of the NHS to engage with patients and carers in the commissioning of services and in service design and provision too.

Section 13Q of the Health and Social Care Act 2006 (as amended) stipulates the involvement of patients and public in commissioning of NHS services in England, and by inference in service planning and provision.

Speaking on 30 September 2011 at the Air Space Conference Centre, Duxford in Cambridgeshire, Andrew Lansley, the then UK's Health Secretary made the now famous quote "No decision about me without me" to drive home his point about the need for clinicians, and the NHS as a whole to involve patients in their treatment plans and the way services are designed and delivered. It is a quote that resonates and often quoted till today, and likely to remain relevant for many years to come. Drawing a parallel between patients in the healthcare sector and the power of airline passengers in cost of ticket comparisons and deciding which airline to fly with, advance seat booking and other prerogatives passengers

---

[78] Speech on 30 September 2011 by The Rt Hon Andrew Lansley CBE on "Right Care 'Shared Decision Making' programme."

exercise, Lansley made a case for more intentional collaboration, consultation, and inclusiveness.

Providing early warning, assessment, and minimisation of potential problems

Engaging and involving users of health and care services in the way services are designed, run, and monitored means that service providers and commissioners get to know what is working well for patients, what needs tweaking, and what needs a major overhaul.

Paediatricians looking after babies don't have the full benefit, but at least they have the parents to fall back on for that vital feedback. So, spare a thought for the vets!

Improving public understanding of and confidence in services

The beauty of patient engagement and involvement is that, as patients get to understand what decisions are being made and why, and as they get invited to the table to participate in that brain storming and use their unique expertise as patients to inform the decision-making process, so their confidence in the service grows. If the communication is two-way: you said, we did...or couldn't do because of one issue or the other, trust develops. Growing trust in any health or care provider brings an array of dividends – willingness to answer future calls for participation, confidence in decisions the organisation is making, and a growing community of spokespersons and ambassadors because they see themselves not just as service users/patients but as partners.

Patient and carer engagement, involvement and co-production should therefore be intentional, planned, and strategic – never because 'we are required to do so', as that tends to bring out the box-ticking, tokenistic tendencies. Yes, the law is there to remind us of what must be done (or not done) but the best outcomes of engagement, involvement and co-production can only be realised when genuine efforts are made to obtain feedback about services, even if the feedback makes uncomfortable reading, and when patients are brought round the table as equal partners to discuss new initiatives or plan service improvements alongside clinicians and service managers

Reward and Recognition (R&R)

This is a phrase used to describe the remuneration given or allocated to patient representatives and carers who engage with service providers or commissioners in developing or improving services.

Examples of work for which R&R may be paid include reviewing of letters or other documents such as policies and strategy documents, participating in focus groups, and attending meetings.

These payments are made to demonstrate appreciation for the time, effort and in some cases, resources used in supporting the work of the organisation.

In addition to the payment of money, other forms of R&R may include the issue of vouchers which can be used to purchase goods or services. Some experts by experience may also request payments to be paid to charities of their choice or decline payments altogether.

At the very least, R&R should cover travel cost, where applicable, and any other expense incurred in carrying out a given task, thus making sure that patients or carers supporting the work of the health and care organisation are not left out of pocket.

In the UK or any other welfare state where monies paid to state benefit claimants may impact on the benefit they receive, care must be taken to ensure that R&R payments does not cause experts by experience who are receiving state benefits to go over the threshold, and thereby become liable to pay tax or have their benefits reduced or in some cases, withdrawn altogether – depending on the volume of their engagement and co-production activities. Guidance should therefore be given to experts by experience on this subject or have them signposted to relevant agencies to ensure the payment of R&R does not become counterproductive.

Getting staff on board

It is not good enough to sing from the same hymn book; you've got to be on page and on cue! This supports the ideology of starting charity from home, achieving internal cohesion and shared goal and so care better for patients and engage the wider public more effectively.

One of the most damaging and unhelpful situation health and care organisations, and indeed any organisation, can find itself is the 'them and us' scenario – management and board on one hand and staff on the other. The polarisation of vision means confusion, the lack of clarity and mistrust. Every scheme or programme management wants to champion would be greeted by jeers rather than cheers, conspiracy theories rather than joined-up action plans. So, what measures can healthcare organisations take to achieve internal cohesion that would enable management/board and the generality of staff to work together harmoniously in the provision of positive patient experience and effective patient and public engagement?

The incentives for health and care organisations to do well in patient surveys, especially national patient surveys are very visible and of high profile. Sadly, same cannot be said of staff surveys. Overwhelming majority of healthcare organisations, particularly in the NHS conduct a whole series of local patient surveys to complement national patient surveys. Again, same cannot be said of staff surveys. There is no doubt that the top priority has to be patients. However, staff must not be the 'poor, distant relative'. Organisations that want to be ahead of the game in patient experience must put enough time and resources into finding out the views of staff and take such views into consideration in developing or amending policies and strategies and in the allocation of resources.

Sources for finding out the views of staff

Surveys

The national staff survey is well established within the NHS for finding out the views of staff on a host of issues, including bullying and harassment, training and development, equal opportunities, fairness of appraisal systems, forms of support available, etc. Two questions are pertinent at this juncture:

To what extent are the findings from staff surveys used in improving staff satisfaction? How often are local, follow-up surveys carried out, to regularly monitor progress of any actions taken? Organisations that score high on these two key questions are certainly on the right track in achieving good level of staff satisfaction.

The scope of this book does not include the 'nuts and bolts' of designing surveys and other data collection tools. Suffice to say that tools that does not allow staff to give comments, in their own words, would have lost a vital opportunity. In general, a combination of qualitative and quantitative methodologies tends to garner more insight than the sole use of quantitative methodologies.

It is equally imperative that staff have platforms and forums through which they can comment honestly and safely, without fear of reprisals.

Service improvement projects and events

Organising events and projects that bring staff together, ideally bringing them out of their normal domains and routines and mixing them with staff from other departments they may not have met is yet another source of gaining vital insights from staff. The more informal and relaxed such forums are, the more likely staff can express their true views – as against 'playing safe' with their comments.

CASE STUDY 13:
'In our shoes' events *(South East England)*

'In our shoes' events were organised for staff in an NHS trust as a follow up to 'In your shoes' in which staff met with patients, their families, and carers to better appreciate the experiences of patients and their loved ones and map out solutions to key concerns.

'Post it' notes were used to scribble key challenges staff in various departments were facing. This was followed by discussions on what can be done to tackle the challenges.

It was reiterated that for staff to be able to discharge their duties professionally and courteously, they themselves need to have a robust support system that would make staff feel they are being listened to, supported, and appreciated.

One of the major concerns highlighted was staffing level and the impact gaps in staffing had on the rest of the team. This in turn, it was noted, would invariably impact on patient experience.

Case study reflections

A happy, motivated and supported workforce is more likely to provide a professional, empathetic, and patient-centred service with a smile than a workforce that feels neglected, overworked, and with little or no support and motivation. Hence the saying, happy staff equals happy patients.

Anonymising information from team and one-to-one meetings

Developing a process whereby each department can anonymously pull together common concerns and compliments from team meetings as well as one-to-one meetings is another source of bright light into what could sometimes be a dark tunnel. This is an underutilised source of rich data, as many of the vital intelligence gained through team meetings and one-to-one are often used in silos and for the 'here and now'. What is needed is a system that pulls anonymised data together from across the organisation, with a brief text depicting context. This will help transform staff views in small teams across the organisation to a massive database of staff perceptions and intelligence, allowing trends and themes to be extrapolated.

Good old comment boxes for staff

Despite the explosion in the use of technology for virtually every aspect of what we do in the workplace, there is still room for some traditional methodologies. One of such methodologies is the good old comment boxes which provides an opportunity for staff to make anonymous comments. Considering the fact that most electronic communication are traceable and that many staff within the healthcare sector have limited access to computers, putting pen to paper in the old fashion way may sometimes be the key. Staff also have the option of word processing/typing their comments, to make it even more anonymous. The location of the staff comment boxes also needs to be thought through carefully, to enhance engagement.

The paper comments will need to be collected regularly from the comment boxes. Then the comments will need to be sorted into categories (concerns, compliments and suggestions) to enable themes and tends to be mapped out.

Staff grievances and disciplinary actions

Issues and themes from staff grievances and disciplinary actions can provide another source of intelligence for mainly concerns but possibly for some compliments too. For most staff, complaining about a colleague is a last resort. When this happens, the information provided by the aggrieved staff is often not limited to the core grievance but may also provide insights into other related issues of interest. Same is true of disciplinary actions. It may be useful not only to examine data from grievance and disciplinary actions but to go one step further by asking: is there a wider implication of this singular event? Is a theme or trend emerging?

Exit interviews

Getting the views of staff leaving the organisation or, in the case of big, multi-site organisations, staff leaving a site or division is an often-neglected source of vital information about 'the good, bad and ugly' in an organisation. Those leaving are generally more open in their views and comments, making this a very valuable source of intelligence.

Acting upon the issues raised in both patient and staff surveys, and other sources of intelligence is vitally important for enhancing patient experience. Addressing concerns from patients and carers without awareness of concerns from staff cannot deliver a lasting and robust solution. As an African adage teaches, it takes the right hand washing the left hand, and the left hand washing the right for both hands to be truly clean. This is true of patient and staff experience and engagement.

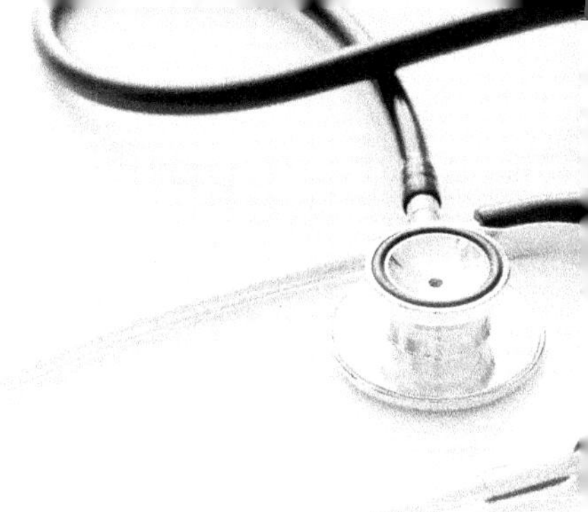

CHAPTER SIX

Drivers of litigation: The impact of empathy and accountability

Why do patients or their families resort to litigation to seek redress? How much is litigation costing the National Health Service (NHS) in England? The fear of litigation has been widely identified as the "evil twin"[79] of litigation – how is this affecting healthcare delivery? Can empathy and accountability in the management of complaints and patient safety incidents influence patients' or their carers/families' propensity to take legal action against the NHS or indeed any other health care providers? What other measures can help reduce the cost of litigation?

[79] F Furedi and J Bristow are authors of 'The Social Cost of Litigation' (2012)

The cost implications of clinical negligence are now very significant. Between 2006-07 and 2019-20 the annual cost to the public purse quadrupled from £600 million to £2.3 billion. The total liabilities which stood at £9 billion in 2007 now amount to more than £82 billion.[80]

NHS litigation reform
House of Commons Committee report
13th Report of Session 2021-22

Patients and their families often resort to litigation to seek redress for what they consider a dysfunctional service or avoidable harm for an array of reasons. One reason is the conviction that the healthcare provider is being 'economical with the truth' or covering up something. Closely related to this is the failure to apologise and show empathy for the experience they expressed dissatisfaction about. A serious harm or 'never event'[81] such as surgical blunders is one of the leading causes of litigation in healthcare.

Litigation is a route taken by a very tiny minority of patients, relatives/carers who felt aggrieved. The vast majority of patients and carers still use the complaints process, the patient safety or serious incident investigation, or the claims process and reach an amicable resolution with the healthcare organisation concerned.

The principal body responsible for managing indemnity schemes for the NHS, on behalf of the UK Secretary of State for Health and Social Care, is NHS Resolution – the operating name for the

---

[80] 'NHS litigation reform' – UK Parliament (2022)

[81] Entirely preventable serious incidents such as wrong site surgery or foreign object retained in the body after surgery. See appendix for the revised list of Never Events list (published by NHS Improvement in 2018 and revised in 2021 by NHS England.

National Health Service Litigation Authority (NHSLA). Stating the reasons why people make claims for compensation from the NHS, NHS Resolution identifies "clinical errors, employee injuries and accidents on NHS premises."[82]

Vincent, Phillips and Young[83] (1994) conducted an empirical study to find out why patients and carers take legal action against the healthcare provider and surveyed 227 patients and relatives in the process. They found out that the decision to opt for litigation was not always due only to any injuries the patient may have suffered but significantly also due to lack of sensitive response and poor communication after the incident.

Vincent, Phillips, and Young (1994) identified four main themes from their study on why patients and their loved ones resort to legal action. These include standard of care concerns with a key aim of preventing recurrence, the quest for a detailed understanding of how and why the incident occurred, obtaining financial compensation to cover past losses and for future care, and lastly to make the organisation or service provider accept responsibility for the incident and be accountable.

In her piece in the European Journal of Health Law, Tumelty[84] (2020) focuses on the role of apologies in medical negligence claims and disputes. Using analysis drawn from a study conducted in Ireland, Tumelty critiques the role of apologies in such disputes and concluded that legislative protection of apologies will not on its

---

[82] www.resolution.nhs.uk – 'What we do' (Accessed 20 July 2021)

[83] The Lancet, vol 343, Issue 8913, June 1994.

[84] Mary-Elizabeth Tumelty's article is titled 'Medical Negligence Litigation and Apologies: An Empirical Examination', July 2020.

own make apology an effective tool in the armoury of health care providers seeking to resolve medical negligence claims.

How much is litigation costing the NHS in England? What measures can help reduce the cost?

At an NHS trust in East Midlands, BBC News reported that at least seven preventable baby deaths occurred between 2015 – 2020 at that one NHS trust alone. In that same period, Buchanan (2021) reported that £60 million was paid out in damages relating to 20 baby and mother deaths as well as 40 cases of brain damage.[85]

In 2017/18, less than a third of all claims resulted in litigation, with less than 1% ending up in full trial. Negotiations through correspondence, meetings between parties and formal mediation were platforms through which vast majority of claims were settled.[86] In 2019/20, 71.5% of claims were resolved outside the courts system, with the figure increasing even further to 74.7% in 2020/21 financial year, as reported by NHS Resolution.[87]

It is however worth bearing in mind that even a tiny fraction of claims ending up in full blown litigation still results into a huge financial burden for the NHS, hence the need to do more in using alternative platforms and processes in reaching amicable resolutions.

---

[85] https://www.bbc.co.uk/news/uk-39807683 (Accessed: 22 July 2021)

[86] Ditto – 'Claims Management' (About) (Accessed 20 July 2021)

[87] NHS Resolution Annual Report and Accounts, 2020/21.

Furedi and Bristow[88] (2012) noted:

"Far from increasing safety and accountability, today's culture of litigation has resulted in significant costs to the quality of services, the experiences of those who use them, and the role of professionals."

In his welcome address in the 2021/22 Annual Reports of NHS Resolution, Mike Pinkerton (Interim Chair) noted that:

"… the cost to the public purse of responding to clinical negligence continued to rise over the last year with damages payments under secondary care clinical schemes increasing by 10.3% to £1.775 billion and claimant and NHS legal costs also rising, the latter at a slower rate than the former."[89]

Quoting another significant data, Pinkerton also said in his welcome address:

"… claims arising from incidents in 2021/22, which is £13.3 billion, a figure we have referred to previously as the "annual cost of harm"[90].

Pinkerton went on to comment on the staggering £13.3 billion bill:

"The key contributor to this is the cost of maternity related claims which make up 62% of secondary care clinical claims by value and 12% by volume, hence our continued focus on supporting improvements in maternity care…"[91]

---

[88] Furedi, F. and J Bristow, J. are authors of 'The Social Cost of Litigation' (2012).

[89] NHS Resolution Annual Report and Accounts, 2021/22

[90] Ditto

[91] Ditto

Can anything be done to stem the fast flow of litigation? If litigation was intended by an aggrieved patient to jolt the healthcare provider into patient-centred actions and positive clinical outcomes, then a question looms large as to whether this approach is working, considering the fast rise in the litigation bill. The litigation cost incurred by a healthcare organisation such as a hospital means less money for the provision of services.

CASE STUDY 14:
Cooking up a claim will get your fingers burnt
(East Midlands, England)

A fraudulent claim of clinical negligence against an NHS trust in the East Midlands culminated in a jail term of about seven months for the claimant. The sentence was given in court on 2 July 2021. The Judge noted that the claimant's "actions were so serious that only an immediate custodial sentence was appropriate."[92]

The Judge found that the claimant had intentionally exaggerated his disabilities, with planning over a number of years, with the intent of having a favourable outcome in the clinical negligence claim brought against the trust.

The case relates to treatment received by the claimant in August 2013 which led him to allege that the NHS trust failed to diagnose and treat Cauda Equina Syndrome (CES) which is a spinal condition that would normally require an urgent surgery. The trust admitted liability about three years later, in April 2016, paving the way for

[92] Statement made by His Honour, Judge Lickley, QC, on 2 July 2021

the patient to claim damages. A claim of £2 million pounds was put forward, supported by claims of severe mobility problems requiring the use of wheelchair, and inability to work. However, discreet monitoring of the claimant showed gross exaggeration. Ultimately, the case was settled with a compensation of £60,000. The claimant also had to refund £20,00 initial payment made and ordered to pay the legal fees of the NHS trust.

Commenting on the case and the custodial sentence, Helen Vernon, the Chief Executive of NHS Resolution[93] said:

"These proceedings should not deter genuine claimants, as the trust and NHS Resolution will continue to ensure that those who have suffered injury as a result of substandard medical care are properly compensated.

She went on to add:

"However, this is a stark reminder of the consequences of making a dishonest or exaggerated claim against the NHS."

Case study reflections

Vernon's comment is worth reflecting on, reminding patients and the public at large that whilst it is necessary that those who genuinely suffered harm due to poor clinical care are within their rights to pursue claims and deserve compensation, anyone thinking of making false or exaggerated claims will likely end up as the

[93] The arm's length body of the Department of Health and Social Care which provides the expertise and management of claims against the NHS, ensuring claims are resolved fairly and that lessons are learnt from such incidents and claims.

claimant in this case – custodial sentence, costs, as well as a stain on their name.

Out of court settlement is another approach of resolving clinical negligence or similar claims made against service providers. Over a 10-year period, NHSLA data shows that 45% of medical negligence claims between 1 April 2001 and 31 March 2011 were settled out of court.

Martin Thomas, Chair of NHS Resolution commented on reduction of cases resolved through litigation:

We resolved a greater proportion of claims without formal proceedings (74.7%, compared to 71.5% in 2019/20). We have appointed a safety and learning expert to work in the mediation space, to make sure we capture the insights those claims reveal, for the benefit of the health system as a whole.

Chair's welcome
2020/21 Annual Report and Accounts
Published July 2021

The litigation reduction trend continued in the 2021/22 financial year. Commenting on their Annual Reports and Accounts (2022), NHS Resolution noted that:

"The number of cases resolved continued to increase. 16,484 clinical and non-clinical claims were resolved in 2021/22 compared with 15,712 in 2020/21. The amount spent on claims in 2021/22 was £2.5 billion, compared to £2.3 billion from 2020/21."[94]

[94] NHS Resolution Annual Reports and Accounts for 2021/22, published on 20 July 2022

Helen Vernon (Chief Executive, NHS Resolution) applauded the fall in litigation which she attributed to efforts devoted to dispute resolution. She said:

"...The continued fall in litigation driven by innovation in dispute resolution and a more cooperative approach across the legal market is to be welcomed."[95]

There is another cost to litigation, arguably more damaging - the fear of litigation. This fear often translates to lack of transparency, defensiveness and stifling of innovation.

The fear of litigation, and consequently litigation avoidance, is a potentially crippling problem with huge financial and social costs. In everyday parlance, litigation avoidance is referred to as 'covering your back' and manifests itself in many detrimental ways. Furedi and Bristow[96] (2012) describe litigation avoidance, or fear of litigation as the "evil twin" of litigation culture.

Measures that can address the root cause of litigation

It is evident in light of the above facts and figures that more efforts should be put into tackling the root cause of litigation, in addition to commendable efforts being put into dispute resolution. A combination of the following measures would go a long way in achieving this aim.

Induction and regular refresher training

[95] News release issued by NHS Resolution on the publications of its Annual Report and Accounts for 2021/22. Published on 20 July 2022

[96] F Furedi and J Bristow are authors of 'The Social Cost of Litigation' (2012)

New staff, those returning from long absence such as sick leave or maternity leave should benefit from robust induction (for new staff) and refresher training. Other staff can also benefit. Particularly relevant are guidelines and policies relating to patient safety and various clinical procedures.

CASE STUDY 15:
Gruelling shift for doctor just returning from long maternity leave could not have been helpful in circumstances that led to the death of a young boy *(East Midlands, England)*

The resuscitation of a six-year-old boy was stopped very briefly, between 30 – 60 seconds, in what was said to be a case of mistaken identity relating to a 'Do not resuscitate' order for another patient discharged earlier that day. The six-year-old sadly died, though the short pause in resuscitation was in fact not the cause of death[97], as grossly unhelpful as it was. At the inquest into the boy's death, the doctor who had just returned from 13 months maternity leave acknowledged the long absence from work may have had an impact on her level of readiness for her clinical duties, and the stress of a long shift didn't help either.

This was a complex case but the focus here is to highlight the need for managed return to duty for clinicians after long absence. Refresher courses, revalidation, and other appropriate competency review may be worth considering, at least on a case-by-case basis.

---

[97] Pulsetoday.co.uk – 10 April 2019

Case studly reflections

It is sad for all concerned, particularly the nearest and dearest, whenever a patient dies, irrespective of the circumstances. The family of the deceased deserve and rightfully expect transparency and accountability. The staff involved should also be supported in what must be a devastating blow and a low point in both their careers and in their lives as a whole.

As new tools are being introduced into the armoury of patient safety investigations, lessons learned should be shared as widely as possible, and reiterated as often as possible, to help avoid preventable fatalities and injuries.

Apologies

Saying sorry in a genuine and empathetic way could, in some cases, be the difference between being sued and managing a complaint internally. However, many clinicians and healthcare administrators still find it difficult to say a few words of apology and save the reputation and bank balance of their organisations.

A common error is to equate the giving of an apology to the admission of liability and guilt.

There is no guarantee that an apology would mean an aggrieved patient would not sue – just as there is no evidence that giving an apology would increase the chance of being sued. However, many studies and experience of managing complaints in hospitals show that giving an unequivocal and empathetic apology at the earliest possible time, without the patient or carer demanding for it, reduces the chance of being sued.

Bucco (2006)[98] supports the credibility of using apologies to reduce the chances of being sued. Citing the piece written by the late Dr Richard Friedman, MD[99] for the New York Times, Bucco argued that when a doctor admits fault, they become humbled and human and consequently trust is built, adding:

"A physician humanized through admission of ...faults...is afforded all characteristics of ...human nature, including imperfection. A patient is, thus, less likely to file a grievance or institute a civil action..."[100]

The study conducted by Witman, Park and Hardin (1996) also lend support to the efficacy of apology as a tool for reducing the prospect of litigation. In their survey, they asked patients to evaluate a number of scenarios describing medical errors from the perspective of the injured patient. Almost all the patients (98%) indicated they "desired or expected the physician's active acknowledgement of an error. This ranged from a simple acknowledgement of the error to various forms of apology."[101]

Using focus groups of patients, Gallagher[102] and colleagues came to the same conclusion i.e., apology can help reduce the chance of

---

98 Bucco, A A (2006), 'A Friendly Approach to Reducing Medical Malpractice Litigation'

99

100 ibid

101 Witman AB, Park DM, Hardin SB (1996), 'How do patients want physicians to handle mistakes?'

102 Gallagher T H, Waterman A D et al (2003), 'Patients' and physicians' attitudes regarding the disclosure of medical errors'

a service provider being sued in the healthcare sector. They noted that many patients said:

"... *they would be less upset if the physician disclosed the error honestly and compassionately and apologized... [and]...that explanations of the error that were incomplete or evasive would increase their distress*"[103].

An equally significant point that came out of Gallagher's study was that patients would prefer the apology to be given without any prompting by them.

Impartial and professional complaints handling service

The more robust, impartial, and customer service oriented the complaints service of a healthcare organisation is, the less likely patients or their carers/families would want to explore the litigation route. As discussed in chapter 3, many patients and their families are not very trusting of the complaints process, partly because they suspect the staff in the complaints department would be inclined to 'cover' their colleagues and the NHS trust that pays their wages. This makes it more imperative that the Patient Experience or Complaints department must rise to the challenge and demonstrate fairness and empathy for the patients and the complaint investigator should be given a free hand by management to embark on their investigation of complaints without fear or favour.

A professional, impartial complaints service cannot guarantee that no patient will head for the solicitor's office; nothing can guarantee that. However, a demonstration of empathy, fairness and

[103] ibid

professionalism can ensure a substantial reduction in the number of patients' grievances heading the litigation route.

CASE STUDY 16: "Don't worry … the days of them leaving instruments inside patients are long gone." MRI scanner magnetises forceps forgotten in patient's body three months earlier *(West Midlands, England)*

One of the 750 'never events' unveiled by BBC Radio 4's 'World at One' survey was the case of Ms B, a former nurse who experienced "excruciating" pain when having an MRI scan. Unknown to Ms B, forceps was forgotten inside her body when she had a key hole surgery to remove stones in her gall bladder three months earlier. While having the scan, magnets in the MRI scanner was trying to "pull through her skin", causing a lot of pain.

X-ray had to be used to continue what MRI scan couldn't finish because of the pain Ms B was having, though it still wasn't clear what was going on. Interestingly, the nurse at the diagnostics department was so convinced it couldn't be the case of an instrument left in the patient's body, she reassuringly said "don't worry … the days of them leaving instruments inside patients are long gone".

"*When they found out it was forceps inside me, I was told there was a risk the forceps could have damaged my bowel which is life threatening and that I might not pull through the operation. I just could not believe what was happening to me.*"

Ms B had to quit her role as a nurse.

Case study reflections

What was the 'missing link' that gave rise to the 'never event' in this case? Sadly, the staff charged with the responsibility of counting the number of surgical instruments used before and after the previous procedure 'took their eyes off the ball' and consequently caused avoidable agony and potentially more serious internal injury to the patient. The incident may have led to legal action against the health care provider or payment of financial remedy to the patient. Though robust systems are in place to avoid such cases, human lapses can still happen. This is the more reason for regular briefings and refresher courses to remind staff of processes and protocols, and the consequences of non-compliance.

Raising awareness of the broader cost of litigation

This is a crucial factor in achieving a reduction in healthcare litigations. To implement this, healthcare organisations must team up with the third sector, especially medical charities. Also, there is need to bring on board leading voices in patient bodies. A robust and sustained campaign to educate the public of the dangers of developing a litigation culture which enriches a few while 'milking dry' public funds for healthcare provision needs to be prioritised. The campaign should also highlight the likely damage to innovation and the fuelling of defensive medicine. Any awareness initiatives should also recognise that preventable errors that leads to harm or fatalities deserve to be investigated fully and patients/families adequately compensated, ideally out of court with NHS Resolution and the NHS trust concerned playing key roles.

President George W Bush used his speech at the Medical College of Wisconsin on 11 February 2002 to raise awareness of this issue. He noted:

"...we should be serving the interests of the patients, not the self-interest of trial lawyers...There will always be matters that can and will be resolved in a courtroom. But...needless litigation does incredible harm to our health care system. It costs everyone time and money...and can destroy the bond of trust between physician and patient.... It is really important to remember that we want to help doctors to heal, not encourage lawyers to sue.".[104]

There is no doubt that the NHS, launched in England on 5 July 1948[105] is one of the most valued British institutions, providing the much-needed free service at the point of delivery. Private healthcare thrives too, primarily to avoid the long waiting list that NHS service may present. The opening ceremony of 2012 London Olympics reinforces the adulation of the British public for the NHS.

There is therefore the urgent need to start a planned and sustained awareness campaign of educating the public that, if this 75-year-old much loved institution is to continue the provision of quality health care services into the 22nd century, then the culture of litigation has to change.

---

[104] http://www.whitehouse.gov/news/releases/2002/02/20020211-4.html. (Accessed 15 September 2022)

[105] http://www.nhs.uk/NHSEngland/thenhs/nhshistory/Pages/NHShistory1948.aspx (Accessed 15 September 2022)

It is important to reiterate that what is being proposed is not to impose a ban on compensation for medical negligence and other errors on the part of clinicians and healthcare administrators. The point being made is the need to substitute a litigation culture for a culture that promotes the following:

- High clinical and safety standards, backed by regular training and refresher workshops
- Transparency and giving of apology without being prompted when mistakes are made
- Robust, fair, and patient-centred complaint and patient safety investigation processes
- Public awareness of the cost of litigation and fear of litigation and their damaging effect on the provision of quality healthcare

Considering the fact that the most efficient processes, guidelines and structures cannot provide full proof immunity against human error, a compensation system that is fair and proportionate should be in place, thereby reducing reliance on tort litigation for making personal injury claims. Unfortunately, the clinical negligence system has so far eluded efforts to turn it into relics of legal history. The progress being reported in recent years by NHS Resolution in reducing litigation through dispute resolution is very much welcome. However, if prevention is better than cure, then more resources should be put into tackling the underlying factors that make patients and their families feel they have done enough of 'running around' and needed to pass the baton to their lawyers.

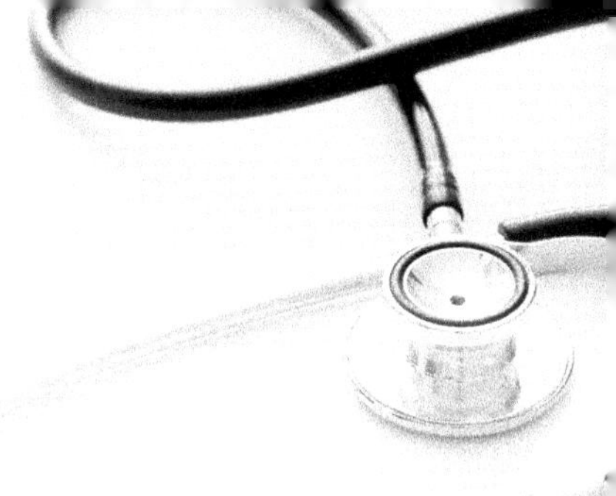

CHAPTER SEVEN

Delivering patient experience in a covid pandemic era

What challenges did the COVID-19 pandemic pose to health care delivery, particularly from a patient experience perspective? What actions were taken to address the challenges posed.

Lastly, what lessons were learned, and still being learned, from the pandemic experience by hospital administrators, including patient experience teams.

From watching real life devastation in China unfold on TV to the once-in-a-century catastrophe criss-crossing countries and continents - it all felt like the biblical Armageddon.

News of SARS-COV-2 (later named COVID-19 by WHO[106]) first broke out in the UK, and probably about the same time across the globe when cases were reported in December 2019 in Wuhan, Hubei province in China. Chinese epidemiologists at the Chinese Centre for Disease Control and Prevention (CCDC) then referred to COVID-19 as 'pneumonia of an unknown cause'.[107]

The UK's direct exposure to COVID-19 happened on 29 January 2020 when two Chinese nationals staying at a York hotel fell ill. Less than two months later, with reports of deaths across different continents, WHO declared a pandemic on 11 March 2020.

The UK's Office for National Statistics (ONS) reported that 67,350 (11.5%) of all deaths in 2021 in England and Wales were due to COVID-19. This figure was lower in 2020 with 73,766 (12.1%) of all deaths recorded caused by COVID-19.[108]

Similar to government emergency policy across many countries, lockdown was introduced which restricted freedom of movement and a number of other social liberties, including restricted visits to hospitals, care and nursing homes in a bid to curb the spread of the

[106] World Health Organisation

[107] British Foreign Policy Group https://bfpg.co.uk/2020/04/covid-19-timeline/ (Accessed 11/03/23)

[108] 'Deaths due to COVID-19, registered in England and Wales: 2021' (Release date: 1 July 2022)

virus. The situation also led to massive scarcity of food items such as eggs and regular household items such as toilet rolls.

Challenge 1

Curbing spread of COVID-19 infections in hospitals

Actions and learning from Challenge 1

Checking temperature and handing out free hand sanitisers and face masks, done mostly by volunteers

This was perhaps the most visible to patients and the wider public of the measures taken to limit the spread of the virus by providers of healthcare at all levels, including GP practices, hospitals, care homes, and nursing homes.

Hospitals used their volunteers and recruited more to help with this task. Many airlines, with flights suspended due to Covid also redeployed their staff temporarily to support hospitals in checking temperature of patients and visitors, handing out face masks, and squeezing out hand gel to the palms of patients and visitors. These measures helped a great deal in limiting the spread of Covid in health facilities such as hospitals.

Inpatients' status classification and increased frequency of tests

Patients were tested for COVID-19 on admission. Those found to have the virus were put in the red zone and immediately separated from other patients while those that tested negative were placed in the green zone as they were deemed to have no risk of infecting other patients or staff. There was the third group, in the amber zone. These were patients whose tests were inconclusive, so they were kept away from those in the green and red zones while their COVID-19 tests were repeated.

Tests were repeated often for all groups, as someone declared Covid-free on day one may get infected or manifest symptoms of the virus a few days later.

Stopping routine visits to patients by friends and family

Routine visits to patients by friends and family were stopped and only permitted in exceptional circumstances and putting in place infection prevention and control (IPC) protocols such as the visitor having a negative Covid test result, undergoing temperature checks and using hand sanitiser and face mask.

In addition, hospital services such as the Complaints and PALS[109] office which were normally opened to patients and visitors were closed to avoid spread of the virus.

Learning includes better appreciation of prevention and containment, as well as timely, empathetic, and transparent communication with patients' families and carers.

---

[109] Patient Advice and Liaison Service

CASE STUDY 17: Hospital set up Family Liaison Team to help facilitate communication between patients and their loved ones during the COVID-19 pandemic *(East of England)*

The stoppage of routine visits to inpatients meant that friends and families were cut off from their loved ones receiving care in hospitals. To ensure patients can still communicate with their loved ones, hospital staff arranged video and audio calls on request. Staff also provided care updates to patients' next-of-kin and others, with patients' prior consent. Letters and 'get well soon' cards were delivered to patients on behalf of their family and friends. This communication support was made easier through the setting up of a special COVID-19 Family Liaison Team.

The special COVID-19 Family Liaison Team (FLT) was put in place in addition to PALS[110] team whose normal functions include liaising between patients, their carers and families on one hand and hospital staff on the other. The FLT[111] worked in partnership with PALS[112], providing a boost to the support available to patients' loved ones during the pandemic.

The PALS[113] and FLT[114] received many 'thank you' cards by post and compliments via email for enabling and facilitating communication

[110] Ditto

[111] Family Liaison Team

[112] Patient Advice and Liaison Service

[113] Ditto

[114] Family Liaison Team

between patients on admission and their loved ones whilst the 'no routine visits' restriction was in place.

Case study reflections

The initiative of setting up the Family Liaison Team, and the fantastic work they did as an additional resource to PALS, turned out to be a lifeline for many friends and families of patients admitted to the hospital at the time, enabling them to keep in touch with their loved ones as the option of visiting in person was often not possible at the time. It was about a frank assessment of the capacity of PALS (can the service we have deliver what our patients and their families need now?) and deciding that extra resource was needed to meet the unprecedented demand for this service. The service was well complimented by patients and their carers/ families.

Closely related to restrictions of routine visits to inpatients was the inability of friends and families to say farewell to their loved ones who were sadly dying in hospitals. This scenario was more challenging and emotive as the opportunity to say farewell to fathers, mothers, sons, daughters or friends was lost forever. In most of these cases, the patients were not well enough to take advantage of the audio and video communication channels being facilitated by the Family Liaison Team and PALS at the time.

There were complaints from many families who felt hospitals should have done more to make farewell visits possible, as such opportunities can never be regained.

Key learning point regarding requests for farewell visit is the need to apply some measure of flexibility to the visit restriction policy. Such flexibility would require a case-by-case review to determine cases where exemptions can be justified whilst IPC[115] protocols to safeguard the safety of both visiting family members and staff are put in place.

Challenge 3

Managing COVID-19 related staff absences and maintaining continuity of service

A major impact of the pandemic was staff absences and the resultant effect on healthcare organisations and their teams to maintain continuity of service.

Actions and learning from Challenge 3

One of the ways in which this challenge was managed was using a combination of home working, on-site working and hybrid[116] working. In hospitals, apart from staff such as doctors and nurses that needed to be on-site and were classified as essential workers, most other staff had to either work from home or used the hybrid working arrangement at the height of the pandemic. Examples of the latter include staff working in departments such as Accounts,

[115] Infection Prevention and Control

[116] Combination of home working and on-site working. The term became very popular for this working arrangement after non-essential workers were allowed to return to work. Many organisations continue to use this model.

IT[117], HR, and Patient Experience (including Complaints and PALS[118]).

It was also important for staff to learn some of the basic tasks normally performed by colleagues in their teams. The ability to work across desks or service units helped to ease the pressure in maintaining service provision. For example, a PALS Officer learning the work of a Complaints Administrator or Complaints Officer and being able to log new formal complaints on incident reporting/risk management systems such as Datix or Ulysses.

Managers also had to regularly monitor the use of face masks, use of hand sanitiser, maintaining the two metres distance, and other IPC protocols. This monitoring helped to reduce the spread of the virus and consequently reduced the chances of staff being off sick due to COVID-19.

The nurturing of team spirit and pulling together mentally also helped significantly during those dark days at the height of the pandemic.

As things improve and the grip of the pandemic became progressively loosened, the hybrid working model became increasingly popular especially among teams that are not patient facing.

Lessons learned includes avoidance of silo working, promoting cross-training, and continually reiterating the importance of team spirit and common goal.

---

117 Information Technology

118 Patient Advice and Liaising Service

Contrary to initial worries that staff working from home will not be productive, hybrid working appears to be a model that has come to stay, as many organisations can see the benefits for both staff and the organisation. However, more data from the monitoring of productivity levels of the hybrid model is advised, to enable effective and proportionate measures to be introduced.

Challenge 4

Establishing transparency in the investigation of infections that led to patient deaths in hospitals.

In line with the 'Duty of Candour'[119] which was introduced into law in 2014 for NHS trusts and in 2015 for all other health care providers[120] to ensure transparency, the need to be transparent became just as important as the need to be seen to be transparent whilst investigating deaths that occurred particularly at the height of the Covid pandemic.

Actions and learning from Challenge 4

- To ensure targeted focus and transparency in the investigations into deaths during the pandemic, hospitals set up a special team managing 'Duty of Candour' communication with families/carers of patients

[119] Introduced as part of recommendations after the Francis Inquiry into failings at Mid-Staffordshire NHS Foundation trust.

[120] 'Background to the Duty of Candour' – www.cqc.org.uk (Accessed 6 April 2023)

- For the purpose of determining fair and proportionate remedy for the deaths, only patients that contracted Covid-19 whilst in the care of the hospital were included in the investigations
- The dedicated team ensured good communication flow, and that all relevant information were obtained to ensure evidence-based investigation and outcome.

Challenge 5

Moving beyond the provision of emergency and unscheduled care, as most scheduled or planned care and diagnostic appointments were cancelled to enable full focus on COVID-19 emergencies.

In February 2022, NHS England published 'Delivery plan for tackling the COVID-19 backlog of elective care'[121] The NHS cared for over 600,000 COVID-19 patients in hospitals throughout England and administered more than 115 million vaccinations to combat COVID-19 in England.[122] The humongous scale of the challenge posed by the pandemic and NHS response to it meant that certain services had to be cancelled or paused.

The pandemic and the NHS responding with full focus meant that the waiting list in England which was about 4.4 million before the pandemic increased by 1.6 million, bringing the total waiting list to

[121] https://www.england.nhs.uk/coronavirus/publication/delivery-plan-for-tackling-the-covid-19-backlog-of-elective-care/ (Accessed 11/04/23)
[122] Ditto

6 million.[123] The halting of scheduled care increased the likelihood that many life-threatening conditions may not be discovered on time and therefore pose a risk to life. For many others, this meant prolonged physical pain and mental agony.

In addition to those already on waiting lists, it is estimated that over 10 million patients who might otherwise have come forward for treatment did not, including a small proportion of these for cancer diagnosis and treatment. There is enormous uncertainty around whether and when these people will seek treatment, making it very difficult to estimate the impact this will have on both their outcomes and the overall waiting list. However, under a scenario where all these people come forward, and with no further action to increase activity levels above pre-pandemic rates, the waiting list could increase to 14 million patients.[124]

NHS England, February 2022

The cancellation of appointments is often a traumatic experience for many patients and their loved ones, even long before the pandemic. For many procedures, patients may have been told to be 'nil by mouth'[125], may have had to take time off work or arrange child care. So, when advised of a cancellation, most patients find this difficult to deal with, and many contact the Patient Experience team or PALS to raise concerns. Sadly, appointments may get cancelled on two or more occasions, resulting in many affected patients or their relatives raising further concerns or asking that a previously raised concern be escalated to a formal complaint.

[123] Ditto

[124] Ditto

[125] Not to eat or drink prior to a procedure or diagnostic appointment

It is worth adding that patients also do cancel appointments or DNA.[126]

In the pandemic era, the delay was not isolated but on a national scale. Also, the delay was not just for a week or a month, but in many cases over a year, with the disruption, pain, and the likelihood of an undiagnosed condition being so much worse.

Actions and learning from Challenge 5

The catch-up challenge is very much on, with NHS trusts doing all they can to rebook cancelled appointments or make new appointments for planned care. As can be expected, some NHS trusts have more capacity than others in dealing with the backlog and new cases.

Increase public awareness

Public awareness of the need to seek urgent clinical intervention when feeling unwell or noticing changes that are similar to symptoms of any disease condition or infection remains vital. The more people that access diagnostics and treatment, the higher the chances of diseases and infections being spotted on time and thereby saving lives.

[126] Did not attend (missed an appointment without prior cancellation)

Further integration of health and social care services

The more joined up health and social care are, the better the wellness and wellbeing of the people. The integration agenda is central to government policy, enabling data-driven solutions and savings in the long run. The provision of more places in care and nursing homes to ease congestion and long wait of ambulances outside the Emergency Department of hospitals is one example.

Reducing the frequency of appointment cancellations by health care providers

With the worst of the pandemic behind us, there is need to improve the management of appointments, particularly in hospitals in order to substantially reduce the number of cancellations by health care providers. As noted above, appointment cancellations not only create the likelihood of worsening health but also create massive disruption in the social and economic lives of patients and their loved ones.

Raising awareness of the impact of patients not attending their appointments

Patients should be reminded of the impact of not turning up for appointments, either at hospitals or GP surgeries, and that such appointments should be cancelled well in advance if they cannot attend.

In a news release issued by NHS England[127], it was reported than one in every twenty general practice appointments are missed without prior cancellations. With about 307 million of such appointments arranged every year (including appointments with GPs, nurses, phlebotomists, therapists, and others in GP practices), that's over 15.3 million wasted appointments each year. The news release added that the annual financial cost of DNA[128] at primary care level was in excess of £216 million.

The impact of appointments missed by patients is even more dire in hospitals. In a news release published on this specific subject[129], NHS England reported that about eight million hospital appointments were missed without advance cancellation. The news release estimated that about £1 billion pounds worth of appointments were missed in 2017/18 alone, with each appointment costing about £120.

As part of its toolkit, a digital platform known as DrDoctor was funded by NHS England to help improve communication with patients and their carers and make it easier for them to cancel appointments well in advance, so that their slots can be given to other patients and thereby substantially reduce the cost of DNA[130].

In addition to cancellations caused by the Covid pandemic, sadly more cancellations have become unavoidable due to widespread

[127] Published 02.01.2019. https://www.england.nhs.uk/2019/01/missed-gp-appointments-costing-nhs-millions/ (Accessed 12/04/23)

[128] Did not attend

[129] 14/10/2018 https://www.england.nhs.uk/2018/10/nhs-to-trial-tech-to-cut-missed-appointments-and-save-up-to-20-million/ (Accessed 12/04/23)

[130] Did not attend

strike actions by various staff groups within the health service, including nurses, ambulance service paramedics, and junior doctors. In just one week in April 2023, over 196,000 hospital appointments had to be cancelled in England due to strike action by junior doctors[131] which includes not only newly qualified doctors but also doctors with average of 10 years post qualification experience. To make the dilemma even more serious, 86% of NHS Consultants (71% turnout) voted in favour of a two-day strike action in July 2023.

It is significant to reiterate that appointments missed by patients without adequate cancellation notice and those cancelled by hospitals or GP practices not only waste money but also leave a dent on patient and carer experience.

Separating facilities and management of elective care facilities from those of emergency care

The separation of facilities and personnel for elective care from those of emergency care has been advanced as a way of improving the quality of care and reducing appointment cancellations. Long before the Covid pandemic, in September 2007 to be specific, the Royal College of Surgeons (RCS) of England published a report on this very subject[132]. They argue that a separation of services, rotas, facilities, and staff will better support improved service delivery, adding that a separate unit on the same

---

[131] 'Junior doctor strike led to 196,000 cancellations'- https://www.bbc.co.uk/news/health-65305035 (Accessed 19 April 2023)

[132] Separating emergency and elective surgical care: Recommendations for practice https://www.rcseng.ac.uk/library-and-publications/rcs-publications/docs/seperating-emergency-and-elective/ (Accessed 19 April 2023)

premises is preferred to a completely separate premises. The RCS of England further stated that the separation, such as protected elective wards, has the added advantage of minimising hospital acquired infections.

NHS England in its 'Delivery plan for tackling the COVID-19 backlog of elective care'[133] supports the position of the RCS[134]. The delivery plan document states that the physical separation of emergency and urgent care from elective care enables service efficiency as well as boosting the robustness of elective delivery.

Targeted focus on improving access to health care services among minority communities such as the disabled, BAME[135] and LGBTQ+[136].

Raising awareness among the disabled, BAME, LGBTQ+ and other minority communities of the importance of attending appointments and accessing health services when not feeling well is vitally important. Whilst the message is relevant for all, the extra focus on minority communities is vital because they are more likely to have experienced obstacles in accessing health care and may therefore be demotivated to attend appointments or proactively access care when needed.

'Protected Characteristics'[137] as enshrined in the Equality Act 2010 and later amendments seeks to protect nine groups of people and

[133] Published February 2022

[134] Royal College of Surgeons of England

[135] Black, Asian, and Minority Ethnic communities

[136] Lesbian, Gay, Bisexual, Transgender, Queer or Questioning, Intersex, Asexual, and more.

[137] Nine factors identified in the Equality Act 2010 as 'protected'

communities from discrimination. The nine groups are defined by age, disability, race/ethnicity, religion/belief, sex/gender, sexual orientation, gender reassignment, marriage/civil partnership, and maternity/pregnancy.

Language barrier for those whose first language is not English, lack of disabled access, racial prejudice or subconscious bias, homophobic attitude or remarks – these are just a few of the many barriers faced by minority communities. A more dedicated effort may therefore be required to motivate these groups to attend their appointments, cancelling appointments with sufficient notice, and proactively accessing health care when feeling unwell.

The worst of COVID-19 may be over, but the pandemic has left in its trail, in addition to long Covid, a long list of challenges that must be addressed. Many of these challenges are being addressed, as noted in this chapter, but others are still being identified. On 13 June 2023, full public hearings of the UK COVID-19 public inquiry began, and this is scheduled to be completed by the summer of 2026. The inquiry, officially launched in July 2022 derives its powers from the Inquiries Act 2005 and is under the chairmanship of the Rt Hon Baroness Heather Hallett DBE. In June 2023, the inquiry launched its 'Every Story Matters' campaign, inviting patients and members of the public to support the work of the inquiry by sharing their experiences of COVID-19 "directly with the inquiry"[138] So, the story of COVID-19 patient and public experience is only just beginning.

---

[138] https://covid19.public-inquiry.uk/ (Accessed 13 June 2023)

BIBLIOGRAPHY

Aspinall, E. (2020) 'Covid-19 Timeline'. Available at: https://bfpg.co.uk/2020/04/covid-19-timeline/ (Accessed 11 April 2023)

Besley, J (2023) 'Sajid Javid calls for a royal commission into the NHS: 'Dispassionate and honest assessment'". Available at: https://www.independent.co.uk/news/uk/nhs-sajid-javid-royal-commission-b2368861.html (Accessed: 6 July 2023)

Bucco, A. A. (2006), 'A Friendly Approach to Reducing Medical Malpractice Litigation'. Available at: http://www.blogforarizona.com/blog/2013/05/malpractice-litigation-helps-reduce-medical error.html?asset_id=6a00d8341bf80c53ef01910246b325970c (Accessed: 18.08.13)

Buchanan, M. (2017) 'Baby deaths cluster: trust paid out millions in compensation'. Available at: https://www.bbc.co.uk/news/uk-39807683 (Accessed: 22 July 2021)

Buzzeli, L. (2023) 'How the public views the NHS at 75'. Available at: https://www.health.org.uk/news-and-comment/charts-and-infographics/how-the-public-views-the-nhs-at-75 (Accessed: 4 July 2023)

Cherry, K. (2023) 'B.F. Skinner's Life, Theories, and Influence on Psychology'. Available at: http://psychology.about.com/od/profilesofmajorthinkers/p/bio_skinner.htmAccessed: 30 March 2023

Clark, S. et al. (2008), 'Reducing Obstetric Litigation Through Alterations in Practice Patterns'. Available at: https://journals.lww.com/greenjournal/Abstract/2008/12000/Reducing_Obstetric_Litigation_Through_Alterations.14.aspx (Accessed: 14 July 2015)

Commission for Patient and Public Involvement in Health (2008) 'Commission for Patient and Public Involvement in Health has closed'. Available at: https://www.gov.uk/government/organisations/commission-for-patient-and-public-involvement-in-health (Accessed: 3 May 2018)

Department of Health and Social Care (2012) "'Friends and family' test aims to improve patient care and identify best performing hospitals," *GOV.UK*, 25 May. Available at: https://www.gov.uk/government/news/friends-and-family-test-aims-to-improve-patient-care-and-identify-best-performing-hospitals. (Accessed: 20 August 2013)

Dougall, D. (2017) 'Listening to patients, carers, staff and communities…do we care enough?'. Available at: https://www.kingsfund.org.uk/blog/2017/05/listening-patients-carers-staff-and-communities-do-we-care-enough (Accessed: 20 August 2021)

Ferlazzo, L. (2011) 'Involvement or Engagement?'. Available at: https://www.ascd.org/el/articles/involvement-or-engagement (Accessed 8 July 2019)

Friedman, R. (2005) 'Learning Words They Rarely Teach In Medical School: 'I'm Sorry'', The New York Times, July 26 July

Furedi, F, Bristow, J (2012), 'The Social Cost of Litigation', Centre for Policy Studies. Available at: http://www.cps.org.uk/files/reports/original/120905122753-thesocialcostoflitigation.pdf (Accessed 8 August 2013)

Gallagher T.H. et al. (2003) 'Patients' and physicians' attitudes regarding the disclosure of medical errors'. Available at: https://jamanetwork.com/journals/jama/fullarticle/196045 (Accessed: 4 May 2013)

Goodwin, D (2013), 'A tale of two city hospitals'. The Sunday Times, London. 7 July

Goodreads 'Charlotte Bronte – Quotes- Quotable Quote'. Available at:https://www.goodreads.com/quotes/7761786-breasfast-was-over-and-none-had-breakfasted (Accessed 10 July 2020)

Gov.UK (2012) 'NHS Friends and Family Test: Implementation Guidance' Available at: https://www.gov.uk/government/publications/nhs-friends-and-family-test-implementation-guidance (Accessed: 8 July 2018)

Gov.UK (2011) 'Speech: 30 September 2011, Andrew Lansley, National launch – Right Care 'Shared Decision Making' programme'. Available at: https://www.gov.uk/government/speeches/speech-30-september-2011-andrew-lansley-national-launch-right-care-shared-decision-making-programme (Accessed: 6 November 2022)

Hertfordshire Partnership University NHS Foundation trust 'Acronyms and abbreviations'. Available at: https://www.hpft.nhs.uk/information-and-resources/acronyms-and-abbreviations/ (Accessed 15 February 2023)

House of Commons Health Committee (2011) 'Complaints and Litigation'. Available at: https://publications.parliament.uk/pa/cm201012/cmselect/cmhealth/786/78610.htm17(Accessed: 18 December 2022)

Malsher, A. (2013) 'Duty of Candour: patients deserve more protection than simple contracts'. Available at: http://www.guardian.co.uk/healthcare-network/2013/apr/03/nhs-reforms-duty-of-candour-mid-staffs-scandal (Accessed: 1 July 2013)

Mazor, K.M. et al. (2004) 'Health plan members' views about disclosure of medical errors'. Available at: https://www.acpjournals.org/doi/10.7326/0003-4819-140-6-200403160-00006 (Accessed: 3 May 2015)

Komporozos-Athanasiou, A. and Thompson, M. (2013) 'Does the Department of Health Hear Patient Opinions?'. Available at: http://www.guardian.co.uk/healthcare-network/2013/jul/02/department-health-patient-opinions?CMP=&et_cid=40724&et_rid=7471056&Linkid=Does+the+Department+of+Health+hear+patient+opinions%3f (Accessed: 3 July 2013)

Leeds and Yorkshire Partnership NHS Foundation trust (2019) 'Complaints management procedure'. Available at https://www.google.co.uk/search?q=-complaints+flowchart+for+NHS+hospitals+UK&ei=YN6dZIGfOpLqgAabsKbADg&start=10&sa=N&ved=2ahUKEwiBz-uTnun_AhUSNcAKHRuYCegQ8tMDegQIBhAE&biw=1280&bih=544&dpr=1.5 (Accessed: 18 March 2023)

Mcleod, S. (2023) *Operant Conditioning: What It Is, How It Works, And Examples.* Available at: https://www.simplypsychology.org/operant-conditioning.html(-Accessed: 28 June 2023)

Metro (2013), 'Down's Boy, six, is left to die after doctor's mix-up', London, 25 July 2013, p.16

Monger, M. (2019) 'Division of Labour, Part 1'. Available at: https://www.adamsmithworks.org/documents/division-of-labor-part-1 (Accessed: 18 March 2020)

National Institute for Health and Care Excellence (2021) 'NICE impact people with a learning disability'. Available at: https://www.nice.org.uk/about/what-we-do/into-practice/measuring-the-use-of-nice-guidance/impact-of-our-guidance/nice-impact-people-with-a-learning-disability (Accessed: 17 June 2022)

NHS (2022) 'Abbreviations you may find in your health records'. Available at: https://www.nhs.uk/nhs-app/nhs-app-help-and-support/health-records-in-the-nhs-app/abbreviations-commonly-found-in-medical-records/ (Accessed: 15 February 2023)

NHS England (2022) 'NHS history'. Available at: http://www.nhs.uk/NHSEngland/thenhs/nhshistory/Pages/NHShistory1948.aspx (Accessed 15 September 2022)

NHS England (2022) 'Delivery plan for tackling the COVID-19 backlog of elective care' Available at: https://www.england.nhs.uk/coronavirus/wp-content/uploads/sites/52/2022/02/C1466-delivery-plan-for-tackling-the-covid-19-backlog-of-elective-care.pdf (Accessed: 11 April 2023)

NHS England (2021) 'Never Events list 2018 - First published January 2018 (last updated February 2021)'. Available at: https://www.england.nhs.uk/wp-content/uploads/2020/11/2018-Never-Events-List-updated-February-2021.pdf (Accessed: 18 May 2022)

NHS England (2019) 'Missed GP appointments costing NHS millions'. Available at: https://www.england.nhs.uk/2019/01/missed-gp-appointments-costing-nhs-millions/ (Accessed:12 April 2023)

NHS England (2019) 'Overall Patient Experience Scores: 2018 Adult Inpatient Survey update'. Available at: https://www.england.nhs.uk/statistics/2019/06/20/overall-patient-experience-scores-2018-adult-inpatient-survey-update/ (Accessed 14 November 2020)

NHS England (2018) 'NHS to trial tech to cut missed appointments and save up to £20 million'. Available at: https://www.england.nhs.uk/2018/10/nhs-to-trial-tech-to-cut-missed-appointments-and-save-up-to-20-million/ (Accessed 12 April 23)

NHS England (2014) 'Review of the Friends and Family Test'. Available at: https://www.england.nhs.uk/wp-content/uploads/2014/07/fft-rev1.pdf (Accessed 21/11/2020

NHS Improvement (2021) 'Never Events Lists 2018'. Available at: https://www.england.nhs.uk/wp-content/uploads/2020/11/2018-Never-Events-List-updated-February-2021.pdf (Accessed: 16 May 2021)

NHS Resolution (2022) 'Annual Report and Accounts 2021/22'. Available at: https://resolution.nhs.uk/wp-content/uploads/2022/07/NHS-Resolution-Annual-report-and-accounts-2021_22_Access.pdf (Accessed: 26 February 2023)

NHS Resolution (2022) 'NHS Resolution continues to drive down litigation – Annual report and accounts published for 2021/22'. Available at: https://resolution.nhs.uk/2022/07/20/nhs-resolution-continues-to-drive-down-litigation-annual-report-and-accounts-published-for-2021-22/#:~:text=The%20amount%20spent%20on%20claims,billion%20to%20%C2%A3128.6%20billion (Accessed: 12 December 2022)

NHS Resolution (2021) 'Attempted clinical negligence fraud lands claimant with jail sentence and an order to repay damages and costs'. Available at: https://resolution.nhs.uk/2021/07/07 (Accessed:15 July 2021)

NHS Resolution (2021) 'Annual Report and Accounts 2020/21'. Available at: https://resolution.nhs.uk/wp-content/uploads/2021/07/Annual-report-and-accounts-2020-2021-WEB-1.pdf (Accessed: 26 February 2023)

Office for National Statistics (2022) 'Deaths due to COVID-19, registered in England and Wales: 2021'. Available at: https://www.ons.gov.uk/peoplepopulationandcommunity/birthsdeathsandmarriages/deaths/articles/deathsregisteredduetocovid19/2021 (Accessed: 10 September 2022)

Parliamentary and Health Service Ombudsman (2016). 'Quality of NHS complaints investigations – The statutory Duty of Candour'. Available at: https://publications.parliament.uk/pa/cm201617/cmselect/cmpubadm/94/9407.htm#:~:text=However%2C%20the%20PHSO%20report%20noted%20that%20NHS%20staff,relevant%20staff%20on%20the%20Duty%20of%20Candour%E2%80%9D.%20109 (Accessed:18 October 2018)

Parliamentary and Health Service Ombudsman (2014) *Hospital fails to diagnose breast cancer – A report by the Health Service Ombudsman on an investigation into West Hertfordshire Hospitals NHS trust.* London: Her Majesty's Stationery Office.

Parliamentary and Health Service Ombudsman (2011). 'Care and compassion? Report of the Health Service Ombudsman on ten investigations into NHS care of older people'. Available at: https://www.ombudsman.org.uk/sites/default/files/201610/Care%20and%20Compassion.pdf (Accessed: 18 October 2018)

Parliament.UK (2007) 'Recent history of Patient and Public Involvement'. Available at:https://publications.parliament.uk/pa/cm200607/cmselect/cmhealth/278/27806.htm(Accessed: 3 May 2021)

Powell, R A and Single, H M (1996), 'Focus Groups', International Journal for Quality in Health Care, vol.8, issue 5, pp. 499-504. Available at: http://doi.org/10.1093/intqhc/8.5.499 (Accessed: 18 September 2020)

Pulse (2019) 'Bawa-Garba: timeline of a case that has rocked medicine'. Available at: https://www.pulsetoday.co.uk/analysis/regulation/bawa-garb a-timeline-of-a-case-that-has-rocked-medicine/ (Accessed: 8 November 2020)

Reeves, R. (2013) '*The friends and family test is a foe to the NHS*'. Available at:https://www.hsj.co.uk/comment/the-friends-and-family-test-is-a-foe-to-the-nhs/5061906.article (Accessed: 25 February 2015)

Robbernnolt, J. K. (2008) 'Apologies and medical error'. Available at: http://www.ncbi.nlm.nih.gov/pmc/articles/PMC2628492/ (Accessed: 19 August 2015)

Spiteri, G. et al. (2020) 'First cases of coronavirus disease 2019 (COVID-19) in the WHO European Region, 24 January to 21 February 2020'. Available at: https://www.eurosurveillance.org/content/10.2807/1560- 7917.ES.2020.25.9.2000178 (Accessed: 11 March 2023)

The Beryl Institute (no date) 'Defining Patient and Human Experience'. Available at: https://theberylinstitute.org/defining-patient-experience/#:~:text=We%20define%20the%20patient%20experience,across%20the%20continuum%20of%20care (Accessed: 3 May 2019)

Care Quality Commission (2022) 'Updated guidance on meeting the duty of candour'. Available at: https://www.cqc.org.uk/news/stories/updated-guidance-meeting-duty candour#:~:text=The%20duty%20of%20candour%20was,a%20statutory%20duty%20of%20candour (Accessed:12 November 2022)

The Care Quality Commission (2019) 'NHS Patient Survey Programme. 2018 Adult Inpatient Survey: Quality and Methodology Report'. Available at https://www.cqc.org.uk/sites/default/files/20190620_ip18_qualitymethodology.pdf (Accessed: 12 December 2021)

The Care Quality Commission (2015) 'CQC welcomes Kings Fund report on patient experience in hospitals over the last 10 years'. Available at: https://www.cqc.org.uk/news/releases/cqc-welcomes-kings-fund-report-patient-experience-hospitals-over-last-ten-years (Accessed: 5 November 2022)

The Lancet (1994) 'Why do people sue doctors? A study of patients and relatives taking legal action'. Available at: https://www.sciencedirect.com/science/article/abs/pii/S0140673694930627 (Accessed:7 January 2014)

The Press Association (2013) '750 people suffer 'never events'' Available at: http://www.hsj.co.uk/5058465.article?referrer=e2 (Accessed: 10 May 2017)

The Royal College of Surgeons of England (2007) 'Separating Emergency and Elective Surgical Care: Recommendations for Practice'. Available at: https://www.rcseng.ac.uk/library-and-publications/rcs-publications/docs/seperating-emergency-and-elective/ (Accessed: 19 April 2023)

The White House (2002) 'President Bush Outlines Health Care Agenda'. Available at: http://www.whitehouse.gov/news/releases/2002/02/20020211-4.html. (Accessed: 15 September 2022)

Triggle, N 'Junior doctor strike led to 196,000 cancellations' https://www.bbc.co.uk/news/health-65305035 (Accessed: 19 April 2023)

Tritter, J. Q. and Koivusalo, M. (2013) 'Undermining patient and public engagement and limiting its impact: The consequences of the Health and Social Care Act 2012 on collective patient and public involvement', Health Expectations, vol.16,2, pp.115-118

Tumelty, M 'Medical Negligence Litigation and Apologies: An Empirical Examination', European Journal of Health Law, vol. 27: Issue 4, July 2020, Brill, Nijhoff

UK Covid-19 Inquiry (2022) 'Terms of Reference'. Available at: https://covid19.public-inquiry.uk/documents/terms-of-reference/ (Accessed: 13 June 2023)

UK Covid-19 Inquiry (2022) 'Updates from the inquiry'. Available at: https://covid19.public-inquiry.uk/ (Accessed: 13 June 2023)

UK Parliament (2022) 'NHS litigation reform'. Available at: https://publications.parliament.uk/pa/cm5802/cmselect/cmhealth/740/report.html

UK Parliament (2020) 'The Care Quality Commission' Available at: https://commonslibrary.parliament.uk/research-briefings/cbp-8754/ (Accessed: 11/07/22)

Wales Online (2010) How the 1000 Lives campaign has made a difference to patients'. Available at: https://www.walesonline.co.uk/news/health/how-1000-lives-campaign-made-1924288 (Accessed: 15 April 2014)

Vincent, C et al 'Why do people sue doctors? A study of patients and relatives taking legal action', The Lancet, vol 343, Issue 8913, June 1994, pp. 1609-1613

Witman, A.B, Park, D.M, and Hardin, S.B (2005), 'How do patients want physicians to handle mistakes? A survey of internal medicine patients in an academic setting" Available at: https://psnet.ahrq.gov/issue/how-do-patients-want-physicians-handle-mistakes-survey-internal-medicine-patients-academic (Accessed: 8 September 2014)

World Health Organisation (no date) 'Quality of care'. Available at: https://www.who.int/health-topics/quality-of-care#tab=tab_1 (Accessed: 7 October 2022)

Wu, A.W. (2000) 'Medical error: the second victim'. Available at: https://www.bmj.com/content/320/7237/726#:~:text=Many%20errors%20are%20built%20into,they%20are%20the%20second%20victims. (Accessed: 18 August 2013)

APPENDIX A

2018 National inpatient questionnaire (issued by the Care Quality Commission, England)

INPATIENT QUESTIONNAIRE

What is the survey about?

This survey is about your **most recent** experience as an **inpatient** at the NHS hospital named in the letter enclosed with this questionnaire.

Who should complete the questionnaire?

The questions should be answered by the person named on the front of the envelope. If that person needs help to complete the questionnaire, the answers should be given from their point of view – not the point of view of the person who is helping.

Completing the questionnaire

For each question please cross ☒ clearly inside one box using a black or blue pen. For some questions you will be instructed that you may cross more than one box.

Sometimes you will find the box you have crossed has an instruction to go to another question. By following the instructions carefully you will miss out questions that do not apply to you.

Don't worry if you make a mistake; simply fill in the box ■ and put a cross ☒ in the correct box.

Please **do not** write your name or address anywhere on the questionnaire.

Questions or help?

If you have any queries about the questionnaire, please call our helpline number:

<Insert helpline number here>

Taking part in this survey is voluntary. **Your answers will be treated in confidence.**

1

Please remember, this questionnaire is about your **most recent** stay at the hospital named in the accompanying letter.

ADMISSION TO HOSPITAL

1. Was your most recent hospital stay planned in advance or an emergency?

   1 ☐ Emergency or urgent → **Go to 2**

   2 ☐ Waiting list or planned in advance → **Go to 5**

   3 ☐ Something else → **Go to 2**

THE ACCIDENT & EMERGENCY DEPARTMENT

2. When you arrived at the hospital, did you go to the A&E Department (also known as the Emergency Department, Casualty, Medical or Surgical Admissions unit)?

   1 ☐ Yes → **Go to 3**

   2 ☐ No → **Go to 5**

3. While you were in the A&E Department, how much information about your condition or treatment was given to you?

   1 ☐ Not enough

   2 ☐ Right amount

   3 ☐ Too much

   4 ☐ I was not given any information about my treatment or condition

   5 ☐ Don't know / can't remember

4. Were you given enough privacy when being examined or treated in the A&E Department?

   1 ☐ Yes, definitely

   2 ☐ Yes, to some extent

   3 ☐ No

   4 ☐ Don't know / can't remember

EMERGENCY & URGENTLY ADMITTED PATIENTS, now please go to Question 9

WAITING LIST & PLANNED ADMISSION PATIENTS, please continue to Question 5

WAITING LIST OR PLANNED ADMISSION

5. When you were referred to see a specialist, were you offered a choice of hospital for your **first hospital appointment?**

   1 ☐ Yes

   2 ☐ No, but I would have liked a choice

   3 ☐ No, but I did not mind

   4 ☐ Don't know / can't remember

6. How do you feel about the length of time you were on the waiting list before your admission to hospital?

   1 ☐ I was admitted as soon as I thought was necessary

   2 ☐ I should have been admitted a bit sooner

   3 ☐ I should have been admitted a lot sooner

7. Was your admission date changed by the hospital?

   1 ☐ No

   2 ☐ Yes, once

   3 ☐ Yes, 2 or 3 times

   4 ☐ Yes, 4 times or more

8. In your opinion, had the specialist you saw in hospital been given all of the necessary information about your condition or illness from the person who referred you?

- ☐ Yes, definitely
- ☐ Yes, to some extent
- ☐ No
- ☐ Don't know / can't remember

ALL TYPES OF ADMISSION

9. From the time you arrived at the hospital, did you feel that you had to wait a long time to get to a bed on a ward?

- ☐ Yes, definitely
- ☐ Yes, to some extent
- ☐ No

THE HOSPITAL & WARD

10. While in hospital, did you ever stay in a critical care area (e.g. Intensive Care Unit, High Dependency Unit or Coronary Care Unit)?

- ☐ Yes
- ☐ No
- ☐ Don't know / can't remember

11. While in hospital, did you ever share a sleeping area, for example a room or bay, with patients of the opposite sex?

- ☐ Yes
- ☐ No

12. Did you change wards at night?

- ☐ Yes, but I would have preferred not to → **Go to 13**
- ☐ Yes, but I did not mind → **Go to 13**
- ☐ No → **Go to 14**

13. Did the hospital staff explain the reasons for being moved in a way you could understand?

- ☐ Yes, completely
- ☐ Yes, to some extent
- ☐ No

14. Were you ever bothered by noise **at night** from **other patients**?

- ☐ Yes
- ☐ No

15. Were you ever bothered by noise **at night** from **hospital staff**?

- ☐ Yes
- ☐ No

16. In your opinion, how clean was the hospital room or ward that **you** were in?

- ☐ Very clean
- ☐ Fairly clean
- ☐ Not very clean
- ☐ Not at all clean

17. Did you get enough help from staff to wash or keep yourself clean?

1 ☐ Yes, always
2 ☐ Yes, sometimes
3 ☐ No
4 ☐ I did not need help to wash or keep myself clean

18. If you brought your own medication with you to hospital, were you able to take it when you needed to?

1 ☐ Yes, always
2 ☐ Yes, sometimes
3 ☐ No
4 ☐ I had to stop taking my own medication as part of my treatment
5 ☐ I did not bring my own medication with me to hospital

19. How would you rate the hospital food?

1 ☐ Very good
2 ☐ Good
3 ☐ Fair
4 ☐ Poor
5 ☐ I did not have any hospital food

20. Were you offered a choice of food?

1 ☐ Yes, always
2 ☐ Yes, sometimes
3 ☐ No

21. Did you get enough help from staff to eat your meals?

1 ☐ Yes, always
2 ☐ Yes, sometimes
3 ☐ No
4 ☐ I did not need help to eat meals

22. During your time in hospital, did you get enough to drink?

1 ☐ Yes
2 ☐ No, because I did not get enough help to drink
3 ☐ No, because I was not offered enough drinks
4 ☐ No, for another reason

DOCTORS

23. When you had important questions to ask a doctor, did you get answers that you could understand?

1 ☐ Yes, always
2 ☐ Yes, sometimes
3 ☐ No
4 ☐ I had no need to ask

24. Did you have confidence and trust in the doctors treating you?

1 ☐ Yes, always
2 ☐ Yes, sometimes
3 ☐ No

25. Did doctors talk in front of you as if you weren't there?

1 ☐ Yes, often
2 ☐ Yes, sometimes
3 ☐ No

NURSES

26. When you had important questions to ask a nurse, did you get answers that you could understand?

1 ☐ Yes, always
2 ☐ Yes, sometimes
3 ☐ No
4 ☐ I had no need to ask

27. Did you have confidence and trust in the nurses treating you?

1 ☐ Yes, always
2 ☐ Yes, sometimes
3 ☐ No

28. Did nurses talk in front of you as if you weren't there?

1 ☐ Yes, often
2 ☐ Yes, sometimes
3 ☐ No

29. In your opinion, were there enough nurses on duty to care for **you** in hospital?

1 ☐ There were always or nearly always enough nurses
2 ☐ There were sometimes enough nurses
3 ☐ There were rarely or never enough nurses

30. Did you know which nurse was in charge of looking after you (this would have been a different person after each shift change)?

1 ☐ Yes, always
2 ☐ Yes, sometimes
3 ☐ No

YOUR CARE & TREATMENT

31. Did you have confidence and trust in any **other clinical staff** treating you (e.g. physiotherapists, speech therapists, psychologists)?

1 ☐ Yes, always
2 ☐ Yes, sometimes
3 ☐ No
4 ☐ I was not seen by any other clinical staff

32. In your opinion, did the members of staff caring for you work well together?

1 ☐ Yes, always
2 ☐ Yes, sometimes
3 ☐ No
4 ☐ Don't know / can't remember

33. Sometimes in a hospital, a member of staff will say one thing and another will say something quite different. Did this happen to you?

1 ☐ Yes, often
2 ☐ Yes, sometimes
3 ☐ No

34. Were you involved as much as you wanted to be in decisions about your care and treatment?

1 ☐ Yes, definitely

2 ☐ Yes, to some extent

3 ☐ No

35. Did you have confidence in the decisions made about your condition or treatment?

1 ☐ Yes, always

2 ☐ Yes, sometimes

3 ☐ No

36. How much information about your condition or treatment was given to **you**?

1 ☐ Not enough

2 ☐ Right amount

3 ☐ Too much

4 ☐ I was not given any information about my treatment or condition

5 ☐ Don't know / can't remember

37. Did you find someone on the hospital staff to talk to about your worries and fears?

1 ☐ Yes, definitely

2 ☐ Yes, to some extent

3 ☐ No

4 ☐ I had no worries or fears

38. Do you feel you got enough emotional support from hospital staff during your stay?

1 ☐ Yes, always

2 ☐ Yes, sometimes

3 ☐ No

4 ☐ I did not need any emotional support

39. Were you given enough privacy when discussing your condition or treatment?

1 ☐ Yes, always

2 ☐ Yes, sometimes

3 ☐ No

40. Were you given enough privacy when being examined or treated?

1 ☐ Yes, always

2 ☐ Yes, sometimes

3 ☐ No

41. Were you ever in any pain?

1 ☐ Yes **➔ Go to 42**

2 ☐ No **➔ Go to 43**

42. Do you think the hospital staff did everything they could to help control your pain?

1 ☐ Yes, definitely

2 ☐ Yes, to some extent

3 ☐ No

43. If you needed attention, were you able to get a member of staff to help you **within a reasonable time**?

1 ☐ Yes, always

2 ☐ Yes, sometimes

3 ☐ No

4 ☐ I did not want / need this

OPERATIONS & PROCEDURES

44. During your stay in hospital, did you have an operation or procedure?

1 ☐ Yes → **Go to 45**

2 ☐ No → **Go to 48**

45. Beforehand, did a member of staff answer your questions about the operation or procedure in a way you could understand?

1 ☐ Yes, completely

2 ☐ Yes, to some extent

3 ☐ No

4 ☐ I did not have any questions

46. Beforehand, were you told how you could expect to feel after you had the operation or procedure?

1 ☐ Yes, completely

2 ☐ Yes, to some extent

3 ☐ No

47. After the operation or procedure, did a member of staff explain how the operation or procedure had gone in a way you could understand?

1 ☐ Yes, completely

2 ☐ Yes, to some extent

3 ☐ No

LEAVING HOSPITAL

48. Did you feel you were involved in decisions about your discharge from hospital?

1 ☐ Yes, definitely

2 ☐ Yes, to some extent

3 ☐ No

4 ☐ I did not want to be involved

49. Were you given enough notice about when you were going to be discharged?

1 ☐ Yes, definitely

2 ☐ Yes, to some extent

3 ☐ No

50. On the day you left hospital, was your discharge delayed for any reason?

1 ☐ Yes → **Go to 51**

2 ☐ No → **Go to 53**

51. What was the **MAIN** reason for the delay? (**Cross ONE box only**)

1 ☐ I had to wait for **medicines**

2 ☐ I had to wait to **see the doctor**

3 ☐ I had to wait for an **ambulance**

4 ☐ Something else

52. How long was the delay?

1 ☐ Up to 1 hour

2 ☐ Longer than 1 hour but no longer than 2 hours

3 ☐ Longer than 2 hours but no longer than 4 hours

4 ☐ Longer than 4 hours

53. Where did you go after leaving hospital?

1 ☐ I went home → **Go to 54**

2 ☐ I went to stay with family or friends → **Go to 54**

3 ☐ I was transferred to another hospital → **Go to 55**

4 ☐ I went to a residential nursing home → **Go to 55**

5 ☐ I went somewhere else → **Go to 55**

54. After leaving hospital, did you get enough support from health or social care professionals to help you recover and manage your condition?

1 ☐ Yes, definitely

2 ☐ Yes, to some extent

3 ☐ No, but support would have been useful

4 ☐ No, but I did not need any support

55. When you left hospital, did you know what would happen next with your care?

1 ☐ Yes, definitely

2 ☐ Yes, to some extent

3 ☐ No

4 ☐ It was not necessary

56. Before you left hospital, were you given any written or printed information about what you should or should not do after leaving hospital?

1 ☐ Yes

2 ☐ No

57. Did a member of staff explain the **purpose** of the medicines you were to take at home in a way you could understand?

1 ☐ Yes, completely → **Go to 58**

2 ☐ Yes, to some extent → **Go to 58**

3 ☐ No → **Go to 58**

4 ☐ I did not need an explanation → **Go to 58**

5 ☐ I had no medicines → **Go to 60**

58. Did a member of staff tell you about medication **side effects** to watch for when you went home?

1 ☐ Yes, completely

2 ☐ Yes, to some extent

3 ☐ No

4 ☐ I did not need an explanation

59. Were you given clear written or printed information about your medicines?

1 ☐ Yes, completely

2 ☐ Yes, to some extent

3 ☐ No

4 ☐ I did not need this

5 ☐ Don't know / can't remember

60. Did a member of staff tell you about any danger signals you should watch for after you went home?

1 ☐ Yes, completely

2 ☐ Yes, to some extent

3 ☐ No

4 ☐ It was not necessary

61. Did hospital staff take your family or home situation into account when planning your discharge?

1 ☐ Yes, completely

2 ☐ Yes, to some extent

3 ☐ No

4 ☐ It was not necessary

5 ☐ Don't know / can't remember

62. Did the doctors or nurses give your family, friends or carers all the information they needed to help care for you?

1 ☐ Yes, definitely

2 ☐ Yes, to some extent

3 ☐ No

4 ☐ No family, friends or carers were involved

5 ☐ My family, friends or carers did not want or need information

6 ☐ I did not want my family, friends or carers to get information

63. Did hospital staff tell you who to contact if you were worried about your condition or treatment after you left hospital?

1 ☐ Yes

2 ☐ No

3 ☐ Don't know / can't remember

64. Did hospital staff discuss with you whether you would need any additional equipment in your home, or any adaptations made to your home, after leaving hospital?

1 ☐ Yes

2 ☐ No, but I would have liked them to

3 ☐ No, it was not necessary to discuss it

65. Did hospital staff discuss with you whether you may need any further health or social care services after leaving hospital (e.g. services from a GP, physiotherapist or community nurse, or assistance from social services or the voluntary sector)?

1 ☐ Yes

2 ☐ No, but I would have liked them to

3 ☐ No, it was not necessary to discuss it

66. Was the care and support you expected available **when** you needed it?

1 ☐ Yes

2 ☐ No

3 ☐ I did not expect any further care or support after I was discharged

OVERALL

67. Overall, did you feel you were treated with respect and dignity while you were in the hospital?

1 ☐ Yes, always

2 ☐ Yes, sometimes

3 ☐ No

68. Overall... (**Please circle a number**)

I had a very poor experience										I had a very good experience
0	1	2	3	4	5	6	7	8	9	10

69. During this hospital stay, did anyone discuss with you whether you would like to take part in a research study?

1 ☐ Yes, and I agreed to take part

2 ☐ Yes, but I did not want to take part

3 ☐ No

4 ☐ Don't know / can't remember

70. During your hospital stay, were you ever asked to give your views on the quality of your care?

1 ☐ Yes

2 ☐ No

3 ☐ Don't know / can't remember

71. Did you see, or were you given, any information explaining how to complain to the hospital about the care you received?

1 ☐ Yes

2 ☐ No

3 ☐ Not sure / don't know

72. Did you feel well looked after by the **non-clinical** hospital staff (e.g. cleaners, porters, catering staff)?

1 ☐ Yes, always

2 ☐ Yes, sometimes

3 ☐ No

4 ☐ I did not have contact with any non-clinical staff

ABOUT YOU

73. Who was the main person or people that filled in this questionnaire?

1 ☐ The **patient** (named on the front of the envelope)

2 ☐ A **friend or relative** of the patient

3 ☐ **Both** patient and friend/relative together

4 ☐ The patient with the help of a health professional

Reminder: All the questions should be answered from the point of view of the person named on the envelope. This includes the following background questions.

74. Do you have any physical or mental health conditions, disabilities or illnesses that have lasted or are expected to last for 12 months or more?

Include problems related to old age.

1 ☐ Yes **→ Go to 75**

2 ☐ No **→ Go to 77**

75. Do you have any of the following?

Select **ALL** conditions you have that have lasted or are expected to last for 12 months or more.

1 ☐ Breathing problem, such as asthma

2 ☐ Blindness or partial sight

3 ☐ Cancer in the last 5 years

4 ☐ Dementia or Alzheimer's disease

5 ☐ Deafness or hearing loss

6 ☐ Diabetes

7 ☐ Heart problem, such as angina

8 ☐ Joint problem, such as arthritis

9 ☐ Kidney or liver disease

10 ☐ Learning disability

11 ☐ Mental health condition

12 ☐ Neurological condition

13 ☐ Another long-term condition

76. Do any of these reduce your ability to carry out day-to-day activities?

1 ☐ Yes, a lot

2 ☐ Yes, a little

3 ☐ No, not at all

77. Are you male or female?

1 ☐ Male

2 ☐ Female

78. What was your **year** of birth?

(**Please write in**) e.g. | 1 | 9 | 3 | 4 |

79. What is your religion?

1 ☐ No religion

2 ☐ Buddhist

3 ☐ Christian (including Church of England, Catholic, Protestant, and other Christian denominations)

4 ☐ Hindu

5 ☐ Jewish

6 ☐ Muslim

7 ☐ Sikh

8 ☐ Other

9 ☐ I would prefer not to say

80. Which of the following best describes how you think of yourself?

1 ☐ Heterosexual / straight

2 ☐ Gay / lesbian

3 ☐ Bisexual

4 ☐ Other

5 ☐ I would prefer not to say

81. What is your ethnic group? (**Cross ONE box only**)

a. WHITE

1 ☐ English / Welsh / Scottish / Northern Irish / British

2 ☐ Irish

3 ☐ Gypsy or Irish Traveller

4 ☐ Any other White background, **write in...**

b. MIXED / MULTIPLE ETHNIC GROUPS

5 ☐ White and Black Caribbean

6 ☐ White and Black African

7 ☐ White and Asian

8 ☐ Any other Mixed / multiple ethnic background, **write in...**

c. ASIAN / ASIAN BRITISH

9 ☐ Indian

10 ☐ Pakistani

11 ☐ Bangladeshi

12 ☐ Chinese

13 ☐ Any other Asian background, **write in...**

d. BLACK / AFRICAN / CARIBBEAN / BLACK BRITISH

14 ☐ African

15 ☐ Caribbean

16 ☐ Any other Black / African / Caribbean background, **write in...**

e. OTHER ETHNIC GROUP

17 ☐ Arab

18 ☐ Any other ethnic group, **write in...**

OTHER COMMENTS

If there is anything else you would like to tell us about your experiences in the hospital, please do so here.

Please note that the comments you provide will be looked at in full by the NHS Trust, CQC and researchers analysing the data. We will remove any information that could identify you before publishing any of your feedback.

Was there anything particularly good about your hospital care?

Was there anything that could be improved?

Any other comments?

THANK YOU VERY MUCH FOR YOUR HELP

Please check that you answered all the questions that apply to you.

Please post this questionnaire back in the FREEPOST envelope provided.
No stamp is needed.

If you do not have your FREEPOST envelope, please return the questionnaire to:

FREEPOST XXXX-XXXX-XXXX,
Address,
Address,
Address,
Address,

If you have concerns about the care you or others have received please contact CQC on 03000 61 61 61

APPENDIX B

Complaints handling flowchart: Process and time management (Based on a 30-day response time)

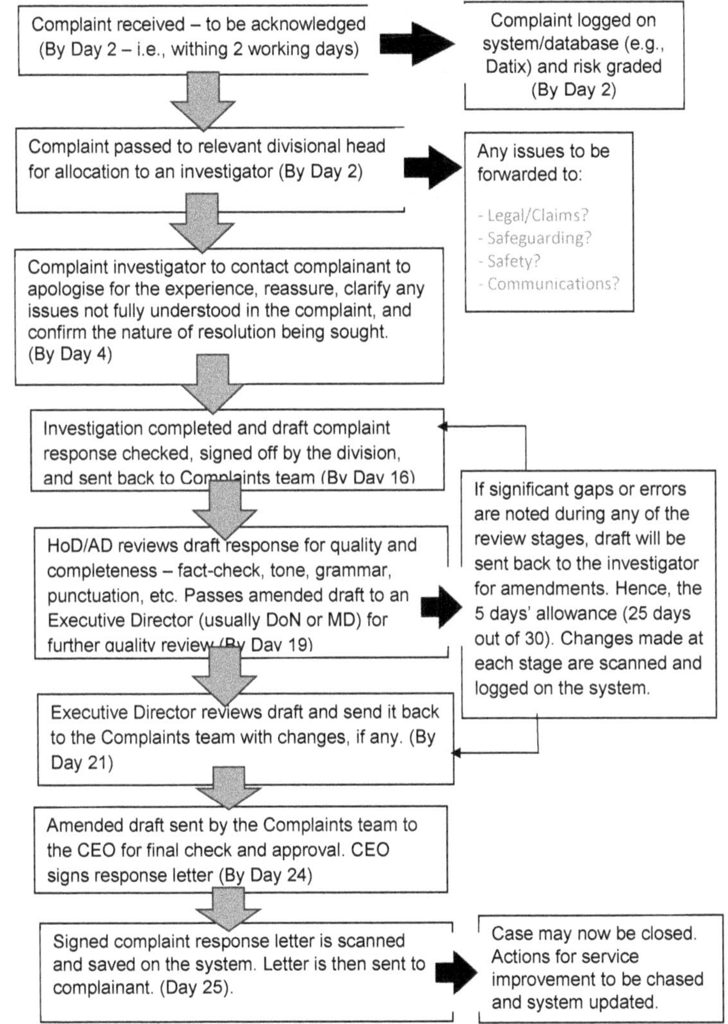

HOD: Head of Department; AD: Associate Director; DoN: Director of Nursing; MD: Medical Director; CEO: Chief Executive Officer

APPENDIX C

Checklist for investigating a complaint and drafting response letter

i) PREPARING FOR THE INVESTIGATION	Tick
Are there urgent actions required to safeguard the patient or to meet the patient's immediate needs? (If 'Yes', contact the Safeguarding team)	
Have you contacted the complainant to have a better understanding of the issues raised and resolution being sought? (If 'No', do so urgently)	
Are there legal implications or threats? (If 'Yes', contact the Legal team)	
Is there any close relationship between the complaint investigator and the person(s) or service the complaint is about? (If 'Yes', a new investigator should be appointed, Contact the Complaints team about this)	
Are there circumstances that make the response deadline impossible to achieve? (If 'Yes', contact the Complaints team)	
Does the complaint relate to other services within or outside the healthcare provider? (If 'Yes', contact the Complaints team)	

ii) INVESTIGATION	Tick
Is the investigation transparent and evidence-based?	
Have all the relevant staff been interviewed/provided statements, including staff who have left the organisation, if appropriate and feasible?	
Is there need to alert internal/external professional standards team? Confidentially liaise with a relevant senior colleague, if unsure.	
Have all parts of the complaint been investigated or addressed?	
Are there parts of the complaint that require specialist knowledge to investigate? If so, liaise as appropriate	
Confidentiality is fundamental. Is there anything or anyone that may undermine this?	
Have conclusions about the complaint been established by the facts presented in the investigation?	
Complaint must never compromise the care the patient is receiving or should receive. Urgently flag any factor that can threaten this.	

iii) RESPONSE LETTER	Tick
Is there an apology in the opening paragraph, at least for feeling the need to complain?	
If response is late, has an apology been given specifically for this in the opening paragraph?	
Is the inclusion of condolences relevant? If so, include in the first or second paragraph.	
Is the style and tone of the response open and honest?	
Does the letter sound defensive? It shouldn't.	
Is the response devoid of jargons or acronyms? If used, have they been fully explained in plain English	
Have you checked the draft for any grammatical, punctuation, or spelling errors?	
Are sentences too long? If so, shorten them. Very long sentences don't read too well.	
Have the names/titles of staff involved been included?	
Does the response include the outcome of the investigation – issue by issue?	
Does the response include the lessons that have been learned as a result of the complaint and the actions that have been taken (or planned to be taken) to improve the service?	

If disciplinary action will be taken, does the response state this?	
Has the investigation manager included their telephone number in the response?	
Are the contact details for PHSO (Parliamentary and Health Service Ombudsman) included towards the end of the letter, advising the complainant of their right to escalate the complaint to PHSO should they feel the need to do so. It is good practice to offer the complainant the opportunity to discuss with a senior manager/Director any aspect of the response letter they are not happy with, in the first instance, before any escalation to PHSO	
Is the letter signed by the Chief Executive, or by another Executive Director delegated by, or standing in for, the Chief Executive?	

APPENDIX D

Abbreviations and acronyms commonly used in health and social care and what they mean

The table below is only a small sample of the commonly used acronyms in health and social care. As evident from this table, some acronyms have multiple meanings which explains why assumptions should not be made about what they stand for. When first used in a letter or document, acronyms should be used with their meanings in bracket next to them and may then be subsequently used on their own.

The full list of acronyms used in health and social care will probably run into hundreds of pages!

A	
#	Denotes fracture (broken bone)
4Cs	Complaints, concerns, comments, and compliments
A&E	Accident & Emergency
a.c.	Before meals
ACHEI	Acetylcholinesterase Inhibitors
AD	i) Associate Director ii) Assistant Director
ADD	Attention Deficit Disorder
ADHD	Attention Deficit Hyperactivity Disorder
AF	Atrial Fibrillation (heart condition that causes irregular, fast heart rate)
AHPs	Allied Health Professionals

AIDS	Acquired Immune Deficiency Syndrome (advanced stage of HIV)
AMHP	Approved Mental Health Professional
APTT	Activated Partial Thromboplastin Time
ASD	Autism Spectrum Disorder (previously PDD)
ASQ	Ages and Stages Questionnaire
B	
BAME	Black, Asian, and Minority Ethnic
BDA	(i) British Dental Association
	(ii) British Dietetic Association
BDS/b.d.s/bds	2 times a day
BMI	Body Mass Index
BMJ	British Medical Journal
BNO	Bowels Not Open
BO	Bowels Open
BP	Blood Pressure
C	
CAFCASS	Children and Families Court Advisory Support Service
CAMHS	Child and Adolescent Mental Health Services
CBT	Cognitive Behavioural Therapy
c/c	Chief Complaint (in medical records)
CCG	Clinical Commissioning Group
C.diff	Clostridium difficile

CD4 cells	A type of white blood cell (see T-Cell)
CDS	Commissioning Data Sets
CEO	Chief Executive Officer
CHD	Coronary Heart Disease
CIC	Children in Care (see CLA below)
CLA	Children Looked After (sometimes used for CIC)
CMHN	Community Mental Health Nurse
CMHT	Community Mental Health Team
CMO	Chief Medical Officer
CNO	Chief Nursing Officer
COVID	Coronavirus Disease (infectious disease caused by the SARS-CoV-2 virus)
COVID-19	Coronavirus Disease (the 19 refers to the year the disease broke out-2019)
CP	Child Protection
CPA	Care Programme Approach
CPD	Continuous Professional Development
CPN	Community Psychiatric Nurse
CPPIH	Commission for Patient and Public Involvement in Health (closed)
CPS	Crown Prosecution Service
CRB	Criminal Record Bureau
CRU	Central Referral Unit
CQC	Care Quality Commission
CQUIN	Commissioning for Quality and Innovation

CSCI	Commission for Social Care Inspection (closed)
CSci	Chartered Scientist
CSE	Child Sexual Exploitation
CSET	Child Sexual Exploitation Team
CSF	Cerebrospinal Fluid
CSU	Catheter Stream Urine Sample
CT scan	Computerised Tomography scan
CVP	Central Venous Pressure
CXR	Chest X-ray
CYPMHS	Children and Young People's Mental Health Services
D	
DHSC	Department of Health and Social Care
DLB	Dementia with Lewy Bodies
DNA	(i) Deoxyribonucleic Acid (genetic information in the cells with unique identity) (ii) Did Not Attend
DNACPR	Do Not Attempt Cardiopulmonary Resuscitation
DNAR	Do Not Attempt Resuscitation
DNR	Do Not Resuscitate
DHSC	Department of Health and Social Care
DoN	Director of Nursing
Dr	i) Doctor
DV	ii) Domestic Violence

E	
EbE	Expert by Experience
ECG	Electroencephalogram (see EKG)
ED	Emergency Department
EDI	Equality, Diversity, and Inclusion
EDS	i) Ehlers-Danlos Syndrome ii) Equality Delivery System
EEG	Electroencephalogram
EKG	Electrocardiogram (see ECG)
EIA	Equality Impact Assessment
EIT	Early Intervention Team
EMU	Early Morning Urine (sample for test)
ENT	Ear, Nose and Throat
ESR	Erythrocyte Sedimentation Rate (blood test for diagnosing inflammation)
EUA	Examination Under Anaesthetic
F	
FAQs	Frequently Asked Questions
FBC	Full Blood Count
FFT	Friends and Family Test
FLT	Family Liaison Team
FOI	Freedom of Information
FOIA	Freedom of Information Act
FOLS	Forensic Outreach and Liaison Service
FT	Foundation Trust

FY1	Foundation Doctor Levels 1 (Year 1 post-qualification)
FY2	Foundation Doctor Levels 2 (Year 2 post-qualification)
G	
GA	General Anaesthetic (use of medicines to create a state of controlled unconsciousness in readiness for surgery, so pain is not felt)
GDPR	General Data Protection Regulations
GERD	Gastroesophageal Reflux Disease
GMC	General Medical Council
GP	General Practitioner
H	
h/o	History of
HAP	Hospital-acquired Pneumonia
Hb	Haemoglobin
HCA	Health Care Assistant
HIV	Human Immunodeficiency Virus
HCSW	Healthcare Support Worker
HDL	High-Density Lipoprotein
HO	i) Heterotopic Ossification (formation of bone tissue in muscle and soft tissue. A common complication of trauma and surgery) ii) House Officer
HOD	Head of Department
HOSC	Health Overview and Scrutiny Committee

HR	Human Resources
HRSS	Human Resources Shared Services
HSJ	Health Service Journal
Ht	Height
HTA	Health Technology Assessment
HWB	Health and Wellbeing Board
Hx	Health history
I	
ICD	i) International Classification of Diseases ii) Implantable Cardioverter Defibrillator
ICS	Integrated Care System
ICU	Intensive Care Unit
i.m/IM	Injection into a muscle
INR	International Normalised Ratio
Invitro	Takes place outside a living body, such as in a test tube
In vivo	Takes place inside a living body e.g., pregnancy
i.v/IV	Injection into a vein
IVI	Intravenous infusion (fluids/drugs being passed into the veins. Drip)
IVP	Intravenous Pyelogram (x-ray test that outlines kidneys, ureters, bladder)
Ix	Investigations (tests, diagnostics)

J	
JCPB	Joint Commissioning Partnership Board
JCT	Joint Commissioning Team
Justa	Part of a word meaning near, as in justaspinal (near the spine)
K	
KS	Kaposi's Sarcoma (cancer associated with AIDS, causes enlargement of blood vessels)
KPIs	Key Performance Indicators
KSF	Knowledge Skills Framework
L	
LA	i) Local Anaesthetic ii) Local Authority
LAA	Local Area Agreement
LAC	Looked After Children
LDL	Low-Density Lipoprotein
LFT	Liver Function Test
LMP	Last Menstrual Period
LSCB	i) Local Safeguarding Children Board
	ii) London Safeguarding Children Board
M	
M/R	Modified Release
MD	i) Medical Director ii) Managing Director
MED	i) Minimum Effective Dose ii. Short for Medicine

MI	Myocardial Infarction
MRI	Magnetic Resonance Imaging
MRSA	Methicillin-resistant Staphylococcus Aureus
MSU	Mid-stream Urine (sample for test)
N	
NCSC	National Care Standards Commission
NFA	No Further Action
NHS	National Health Service
NI	National Insurance
NIHR	National Institute of Health Research
NMC	Nursing and Midwifery Council
NOSO	Prefix meaning sick/infected, as in nosocomial (infected in hospital)
NPS	Net Promoter Score
NRPF	No Recourse to Public Funds
npo	nil peros (nil/nothing by mouth)
NQSW	Newly Qualified Social Worker
NSPCC	National Society for the Prevention of Cruelty to Children
O	
OD/o.d/od	i. Once a day
	ii. Oculus Dexter (right eye)
o/e	On examination

OFSTED	Office for Standards in Education, Children's Services and Skills
OPES	Overall Patient Experience Score (discontinued by NHS England)
OS	Oculus Sinister (left eye)
OT	Occupational Therapist/Therapy
P	
p/c	Presenting complaint
p.c	After food
PACE	Playfulness, Acceptance, Curiosity, and Empathy
PbR	Payment by Result
PCAS	Parenting Capacity Assessment Service
PCN	Primary Care Network
	Penalty Charge Notice
PCT	Primary Care Trust (abolished)
PDD	Parkinson's Disease Dementia
	Pervasive Developmental Disorders (now known as ASD)
PDD-NOS	Pervasive Developmental Disorder – Not Otherwise Specified
PDP	Personal Development Plan
	Practice Development Programme
PED	Patient Experience Department
PET	Patient Experience Team
PHSO	Parliamentary and Health Service Ombudsman

PLACE	Patient-Led Assessment of the Care Environment
PO/po/p.o	By mouth, oral administration
POP	Plaster of Paris
PPI	Proton Pump Inhibitor(s)
	Patient and Public Involvement
PPE	Personal Protective Equipment
	Patient and Public Engagement
PR/pr/p.r	Rectal administration, through the anus
PSW	Principal Social Worker
PREMs	Patient Reported Experience Measures
PRN/prn/p.r.n	As needed
PTT	Partial Thromboplastin Time
PU	Passed urine
Q	
QA	Quality Assurance
QAF	Quality Assurance Framework
QD/qd	Quaque Die (once every 24 hours)
QH/qh	Quaque Hora (every hour)
QIPP	Quality Innovation Productivity Prevention
QSW	Qualified Social Worker
qv	Quantum vis (as much as you wish)
R	
R&D	Research and Development
RCA	Root Cause Analysis

RN	Registered Nurse
RMN	Registered Mental Nurse
RNA	Ribonucleic Acid
ReSPECT	Recommended Summary Plan for Emergency Care and Treatment
RNLD	Learning Disability Nurse
ROSC	Return of Spontaneous Circulation
RSL	Registered Social Landlord
RSU	Regional Secure Unit
RSV	Respiratory Syncytial Virus (virus that causes breathing problems)
RTA	Road Traffic Accident
Rx	Treatment
S	
SC/s.c.	Injection under the skin
S/R	Sustained Release (usually drug release/delivery over a prolonged period)
SaBTO	Safety of Blood, Tissues and Organs
SALT	Speech and Language Therapy
SARS	Severe Acute Respiratory Syndrome
SCBU	Special Care Baby Unit
SCR	Serious Case Review
SEMH	Social, Emotional, and Mental Health
SEN	Special Educational Needs

SGO	Special Guardianship Order
SLT	Speech and Language Therapy/Therapist
SOAMHS	Specialist Older Adult Mental Health Services
SOP	Standard Operating Procedure
SPA	Single Point of Access
SpR	Specialist Registrar
stat.	Immediately, now
STEMI	ST-segment Elevation Myocardial Infarction
T	
t	Time
T	Temperature
t.d.s/tds/TDS	3 times a day
t.i.d/tds/TDS	3 times a day
T-Cell	T Lymphocyte (a type of white blood cells also referred to as CD4 cells)
Tachy	Means fast, as in Tachycardia (fast heartbeat)
TCI	To come in
TFT	Thyroid Function Test
TPN	Total Parental Nutrition
TPR	Temperature, Pulse, and Respiration
TTA	To Take Away
TTO	To Take Out

U	
U&E	Urea and Electrolytes
u.d/ud/ut dict	Ut dictum, as directed
UASC	Unaccompanied Asylum-Seeking Children
UASCH	Unaccompanied Asylum-Seeking Children's Health
UCC	Urgent Care Centre
UTI	Urinary Tract Infection
V	
VAP	Ventilator-associated Pneumonia
vid	See
VLDL	Very-low density lipoprotein
VTE	Venous Thromboembolism
W	
w/	With
w/wt	Weight
WTE	Whole Time Equivalent
X	
X	Unknown factor
X-Ray	Diagnostic test that uses high energy radiation for taking precise picture of a part of the body
X chromosome	Part of a gene that that makes a baby girl (Females have two X chromosomes while males have one X chromosome and one Y chromosome)

Y	
Y Chromosome	Part of a gene that makes a baby girl (see X chromosome)
YOS	Youth Offending Service
YOD	Young Onset Dementia
YOT	Youth Offending Team
YPD	Young People with Dementia
Z	
ZD	Zinc deficiency
ZMC	Zygomatico-Maxillary Complex (a major buttress of the midfacial skeleton)
ZES	Zollinger-Ellison Syndrome (a rare condition in which one or more tumours grow in the pancreas or in the upper part of the small intestine)

www.ingramcontent.com/pod-product-compliance
Ingram Content Group UK Ltd.
Pitfield, Milton Keynes, MK11 3LW, UK
UKHW020132250726
13967UKWH00002B/612